Go Forth to Serve

A History of Henson Scout Reservation,
Camp Nanticoke, 1965-2020

Ken Gerlach
and Dan Shortridge

GO FORTH TO SERVE

First edition July 2020

Book design by Dan Shortridge

ISBN: 9798644071234

Printed in the United States of America

Published by the Del-Mar-Va Council, Inc.
Akridge Scout Reservation
1910 Baden Powell Way
Dover, DE 19904

302-622-3300 | 800-766-SCOUT
www.delmarvacouncil.org
info@dmvc.org

This book is dedicated to the young men and women of Nanticoke
who have hiked the trails, paddled the Marshyhope,
and slept under the stars;

to the Scouters who made this camp their home
and filled it with their time, sweat, and love for so many years;

to the friends who have walked with us,
sharing the burden of irksome tasks
and the joy of fellowship;

and to the friends who were called home
to finish their journey early.

May the spirit of Scouting embodied in this place
and in its people long endure.

Contents

Introduction

The seasons today are anchored in my mind and senses as they were at camp.

The fall floats in with the smell of musty leaves along the trails, the bracing feeling of a breeze off the Marshyhope, and the sounds of Cub Scout chariots racing around the lower loop.

Winter comes with sodden sand that fails to hold tent stakes, getting warm around a campfire circle, and daring a frigid midnight trip to the latrine.

The spring is rebirth, setting up ceremony sites for the Lodge, hearing the crack of rifles on the range, and helping students through a COPE exercise.

And summer, glorious summer, is what we live for, the end and the beginning, the destination of the year.

Summer is the laughter of people hauling tent platforms and four-by-fours; the feeling of sweat dripping down your forehead while teaching under a hot green canvas tarp; and the swelling pride of a teenager putting on the staff polo for the first time.

Summer is gulping down a pint of ice cream in five minutes and drinking Snapple by the gallon; flipping a sailboat in the Marshyhope muck; losing your voice while singing songs under the Big Top; and raiding the kitchen for almond butter and jelly sandwiches at midnight.

Summer is the eternal memory of friends long departed and the cheerful handshake of friendships still to be forged. Summer is the longest day of our lives and the best time we will ever have.

Summer is Nanticoke, now and forever.

In 1996, like many other summer staff members, I eagerly devoured a new publication found in the Trading Post – a history of camp and the area's Native American peoples exhaustively researched by former program director Ken Gerlach. Dr. Gerlach passed away in 2008, but his spirit and words live on in this book, which draws on much of his original research, eyewitness accounts and insights.

This updated history also includes the stories, recollections and tall tales of many of the campers, volunteers and staff members who have been part of Nanticoke's past. It would not be possible without their contributions and generous sharing of their time and memories.

At the time of this writing, we have just learned that there will be no summer camp along the Marshyhope for the first time since 1965, due to restrictions put in place with the coronavirus pandemic. It's perhaps now more important than ever to reflect on where we've come from, consider what may lie ahead, and find new ways to support the camp we have come to love and cherish.

Dan Shortridge
Editor and co-author

A week of camp life is worth six months
of theoretical teaching in the meeting room.

ROBERT BADEN-POWELL

Part One:
Early Years

The Land

Today, five dollars will buy you a patch or a few candy bars at the Trading Post. In May 1963, five dollars bought a camp.

That was the token amount of money that changed hands when Salisbury couple Francis and Bessie Holloway sold 1,485 acres along the Marshyhope Creek and Nanticoke River to the Del-Mar-Va Council. Their generosity and support for Scouting changed the lives of thousands of young people across the region over the course of the succeeding decades.

In the early 1960s, the camp land was uninhabited, with no buildings except a house near the entrance. The Holloways had purchased it in 1959, part from local farmer William P. Coopersmith and part from Tyaskin general store owners Elmer and Edith Cox.

Historical research and early explorations by Scouts and Scouters in 1964-65 turned up evidence of homesteads, small areas where a family would settle down and work the land, chop timber, or burn charcoal to eke out a hardscrabble living. Homestead sites were noted near near the Ababco, Kuskarawa, Crazy Woman, Old Bucket, and Tomahawk outposts, as well as near the Lasher Activities Building and the Longhouse. A 1938 aerial survey photo showed many traces of small fields, and the entire area south of the current Maintenance Shop was open field when camp opened in 1965.

The trail surveys turned up additional signs of what the land had been prior to the Holloways purchasing it in 1959. Old gravel pits were located in the east, near Kuskarawa, and in the west, north of the rifle range. A small family-sized cemetery was also found near Kuskarawa, totally overgrown in 1965. Large circular depressions were seen, up to 50 feet across, marking where hardwood was burned into charcoal, northeast of the parking lot. And the remnants of an old whiskey still were found on a connecting trail between Small Homony campsite and Tomahawk outpost, likely chopped up by law enforcement agents during Prohibition.

Traces of old sawmills from timbering days, possibly as recently as the 1950s, were still found in the northern part of camp. At Lost Mill outpost, a mill was located just above where the Tequissino Trail (red and white) branches west from the Kuskarawa Trail (green and white). At the time of trailblazing, one small shed was still barely standing beside a huge mount of sawdust there. A later archeological report documented a sawmill site along the Marshyhope, located in view of Red Banks along the shoreline between Small Homony and Algonquin campsites. Noted as low and often flooded in high tide, it was unknown to the early founders of camp, including first Ranger Shep Henry.

Decades prior to the camp's purchase, an old county road had gone through the property, passing over the current entrance road and turning sharply north near the waterfront, passing through what are now campsites and going along what is today the road to the rifle range and activities field, where it continued north eventually to El Dorado. The trail from the present trail post to Red Banks in the south was also an old part of the county road system, reportedly used by passenger and mail coaches. When the Ankara Trail (black and white) was cut through in 1964, parts of an old wharf still existed just below water level at Ababco, likely where the mail coach met boats.

The more central area of camp, including south of the pool, the administration building parking lot, and points north, contained very scrubby second and third growth from a devastating wildfire that had swept through some years before. Most of the northern area had been ravaged by timber cutting, rendering most of it unsightly second growth, but dotted with carpets of blueberry and mountain laurel. The campsites from Tamaran and Sandah to Small Homony had been replanted in loblolly pine, as were campsites north to Algonquin. That created an attractive, park-like area.

After the property was purchased by the Del-Mar-Va Council in the early 1960s, the first buildings to be constructed were a tool shed in what is now Tamaran, a water tap and two-holer outhouse in what is now Tiawco, and a two-holer outhouse in the southern part of camp.

The initial plan of the Council was to develop two camps on the property, with the second lying in the southern part of the reservation land. This second camp, which has never been developed, was referred to simply as "Camp No. 2," but the tentative name of "Choptank" had been considered. This was logical, since that is the name of the other major Native American tribe of the county in which the Reservation is located.

One of the most notable features of the camp is Red Banks, a sandy cliff off the Black and White trail accessible only by water and foot. Pottery found there during archaeological surveys dated back to 900 BCE. "Playing on the cliff" was outlawed by Henry because of its erosive effect.

The Nanticoke
and Choptank Peoples

One of the earliest groups of Indians in the Reservation area was the Adena, a culture so far back in history that little is known of them other than through archaeological evidence. Extant in the Dorchester County area between 1000 BCE and CE 200, the Adena had 173 sites assigned to them as of 1976, the most spectacular of which is Sandy Hill just north of Cambridge, Md. This people had apparently been driven by foes from their original homes within the Ohio Valley. Other than the word Adena itself (which is, of course, only a locational name assigned by modern archaeologists), no names concerning this Early Woodland culture exist.

There has been a great deal of confusion over the years about Native American words and names. Most were recorded during the early contact period with Europeans – people who did not speak the languages – and in an age when spelling was a hit-or-miss art. In some cases, the same Indian name was spelled in three different ways in the same early document. The Choptank Tribe's Ababco band is an example, spelled Abaco, Ababcoe, Abapco, Babcoe, and even Abanvo. Major listings in this book are followed by their alternate spellings, if any.

The Nanticokes

European Contact and Conflict

As best we know, the first European to meet the Nanticokes was Captain John Smith, when he sailed up the river in 1608. He called them, on his map, the Kuskarawaok, and identified their towns as Nause, Nantaquak (Nantaquake), Sarapinagh (Saraphanigh), Nanduge, and Arsek (Arseek). The name "Nanticoke" is an obscure term erroneously applied to all Eastern Shore tribes, probably derived from the name of the Smith-era town of Nantaquake. That was likely more easily pronounced by the Europeans than the correct name, Kuskarwaok. Other names for the tribe includes the "Tiawco," while another was "Otayachgo," meaning "bridge people."

Conflicts and land disputes between the tribe and the Europeans quickly developed. A peace treaty was signed with the English in 1658 between the three "kings" of the Choptanks and the "emperor" of the Nanticokes. The Nanticoke leader at that time was Unnacokasimmon, alternately spelled Vinnacokasimmon and Vnnacok Ca Simon. In 1669, he presided over another council with the Europeans, agreeing to allow the modern-day town of Vienna to be laid out. It is possible that the town's name derives from the chief's name.

Other tribal leaders followed Unnacokasimmon after his death in 1686, including Ahoperoon. In 1692, after the latter's death, Asquash, a son of Unnacokasimmon, became emperor, or tyac. Asquash was no friend to the European colonists, who were able to manipulate affairs and name friendlier leaders, Panquash and Annoughtoughk. A peace treaty was renewed with the duo in 1962, and Asquash was named an "enemy of the Province" in 1693. Dissatisfied with the European-favored leaders, the tribe named a new tyac, Felton, in 1697. The Europeans largely ignored this appointment.

By 1697, a European report stated that the Nanticoke nation consisted of 10 towns, some of which had fewer than 20 families. The population had been decimated by smallpox, killing hundreds, as well as malnutrition, tuberculosis, alcoholism, and skirmishes with Europeans and other tribes. A few family groups in each town would have led a subsistence life from agriculture, hunting, trapping, and seafood harvesting.

Eventually, with the European numbers increasing, a reservation was set aside for the Nanticokes – bounded by Chicone Creek to the south, Francis Anderton Branch (now Spear's Creek) to the north, and the Nanticoke River to the east, about 4,000 acres.

The English governor and assembly never fully understood that confining the Indians to land within fixed bounds was inconsistent with the Nanticoke culture and subsistence cycles. The establishment of the reservation thus exacerbated the situation and, in 1705, some of the Indians threatened hostile moves against the whites and a new peace treaty was signed (along with the Choptanks). By this time, Panquash and Annoughtoughk were having their own problems and they acknowledged Ashquash, who had in the meantime capitulated to the English, to be emperor. Ashquash appointed Panquash and Annoughtoughk as "commissioners." Thus it was Ashquash who, along with Winnoughquargo (Winicaco), king of the Ababcoes and Hatsawaps, signed the new peace treaty.

In 1712, Asquash left to live with the Susquehannock tribe in Pennsylvania, leaving Panquash and Annoughtoughk in charge until at least 1721.

Tribal Names

The names used at the Nanticoke/Henson Reservation derive from the Late Woodland Period (AD 1000 to AD 1600) through the Contact Period (AD 1600 to 1799) and were recorded by the white Europeans of the latter period. The English settlers were as ignorant and indifferent to the Indian culture and tribal interrelations as they were about spelling, making modern historical and anthropological reconstruction difficult.

These tribes were branches of the Algonquin (Algonkin, Algonquian) family as recognized by their language. They claimed by their traditions "the Lenni Lenape (Delawares) to be their grandfathers and the Mohegans (Mohicans) to be their brothers," according to a 1966 history of Dorchester County.

"Lenni Lenape" was the Indians' name for themselves and meant "true men" or "real men" in the sense of the phrase "we the people." Most of the names used for Indian tribes and places were given by others; among themselves something like "we the people" not only sufficed for a name, but asserted the superiority of the group.

Life and Culture

The Indians subsisted on gathering, fishing, hunting, and farming. Certainly fishing, crabbing, and oystering were of major importance to the Choptanks and the more southern bands of the Nanticokes. Among their crops were corn, peas, beans, and squash. There was hunting of large and small animals for food (deer, rabbits, squirrels, turkey, doves, etc.) and furs (foxes, beaver, muskrat, raccoon, etc.).

Men kept their faces clean-shaven, using two clam shells as tweezers or sharp stone flakes as razors. Using the same tools, young men removed much of their scalp hair, leaving a small tuft called a "scalp-lock" or "roach" on top. Some shaved one side, letting the other side grow long. Older men let all their hair grow long, parted in the middle to hang down at the sides. They rubbed their hair with animal fat to make it shine. In general, hair was kept in fashions to make forest travel easy, without catching on branches and brush. Hence they wore few feathers or other ornaments and, except for ceremonial occasions, usually wore only one single eagle or turkey feather. The Indians wore no sleeved upper garments. In summer men wore a breech clout and moccasins, perhaps with leggings while travelling. In the winter, a warm animal skin was added, generally simply thrown over one shoulder. Younger men were known to tattoo their skin using a bone needle and vegetable dies.

Leadership

There can be little doubt that the English settlers had little understanding of the Indian culture. The whites' preoccupation with owning land was as foreign to the tribes as, in their turn, the Indian manner of governance was a total mystery to the English. These two misunderstandings led to many of the problems between them. The whites erroneously imposed their own idea of a political model on the Indians, evidenced by the English calling tribal leaders "emperors" and "kings."

These terms bring to the European mind an image of absolute rule by divine right, of men and women ("queens") exercising dominion, through hereditary succession, over lands and peoples. In actual fact, the manner of governance of the Nanticokes derived from their "grandfathers," the Lenni Lenape who lived, as did most Woodland tribes (including the Choptanks) in a confederation of small towns and villages. Their government was a participatory democracy with councils presided over by chiefs (sachems, tyacs, talls, werewances) whose authority came from their powers of persuasion. The term "tyac" or "tall" (emperor) actually referred to a Nanticoke "chief of chiefs." The tyac was elected by a group of clans, bands, or family groups to facilitate decisions affecting those groups, usually on a consensus basis in meetings ("powwows") with the "werewances" (chiefs; "kings or queens") of those smaller units and who were also chosen by their people.

The Choptanks named no tyac (emperor), making decisions among the several werewances/chiefs ("kings") – three at the time of European contact. The tyacs and werewances were thus ordinary tribe members socially who, along with their families, lived in every respect the same way as their people. There was far more of the democratic than the autocratic in Native American self-governance and decision-making. Such a misreading of the powers of these leaders on the part of the English was bound to lead to trouble – and did.

Even more critical, and deadly to the Indians, was the misunderstanding as to the nature of the land. The sustenance and survival of the Indians depended on their need, as hunters and gatherers, to be able to move with the seasons and to meet the challenges of access to several microenvironments as game, seafood (especially oysters and clams), and naturally-occurring plants became scarce. While constrained to remain in certain geographical limits by neighboring tribes, there was no concept of land ownership on the part of individuals or sub-tribal (village) groups. Thus, permanent residence on reservations forced on them by Europeans, whose concept of the land was totally alien, proved antithetical to the seasonal subsistence strategy of the Indians. When they were forced to huddle on what remained of their several white-established reservations, eventual oblivion or removal to another part of the continent became inevitable.

Towns

In addition to the towns mentioned by John Smith during his 1608 exploration of the Nanticoke River, Lord Baltimore in a 1678 letter referred to Puckamee on the southeast side of the Nanticoke River in Somerset County and to Chiccacone (Chicone, Chicacone) on the northwest side of the River in Dorchester County. Also on the south side was a place referred to as "Emperor's Landing," possibly a canoe landing for a town near present-day Vienna. Unfortunately, there is no map showing the locations of wigwams or the exact locations of these villages.

The Winnasoccum Rebellion

In the late 1730s and early 1740s, abetted by the French, groups of Native Americans under the leadership of the Shawnee (Shawan) chief Tecumseh were urged to join their efforts to overthrow the English and to reclaim their lands. A delegation from this league persuaded a number of local Indians to join this insurrection.

In 1742, still without an emperor, a number of Nanticokes planned to rise up and, in one night, to overthrow and massacre the Europeans. To this end, they had gathered with their women and children on a small island called Winnasoccum in the middle of the Pocomoke Swamp. They had built a 20 by 25 foot lodge house as an armory and had stockpiled several guns, ammunition, and poison- tipped arrows. Some Indians friendly to the English, including the Choptank Indian Jemmy Smallhomony, informed the whites of the plot. Prompt defenses were made all along the frontier, and the rebellion was averted.

According to Smallhomony's deposition of June 25, 1742, the local Indians were to have been assisted by some 500 of the Shawnees and Northern Indians and at about the same time the French, with the assistance of other Indians were to attack in Maryland and Pennsylvania from the north. The Nanticokes and their Shawnee allies were to cut off the English in "Somerset and Dorset" and to extend their conquest upwards till they had joined the other Indians and the French.

Exodus

Through these last difficult years, the only thing that kept many Nanticokes in Maryland was their lucrative fur trade with the English entrepreneurs. But the Indians became increasingly dissatisfied, especially after the failure of the rebellion of 1742, and in 1744, the Nanticokes obtained permission from the British, gathered up their dead ancestors and other sacred relics and moved out of the Maryland area to settle in northern Pennsylvania near the present town of Towanda, a name derived from the Indian word "Towandeunk," literally meaning "Where we bury our dead."

The migration to the north took place beginning in 1743 and 1744 by water up the Chesapeake Bay, the Susquehanna River, and by 1753, to the Binghamton area of New York, finally arriving at the Nanticoke Refuge at Fort Niagara between the years 1778 and 1851. A few scattered families of Nanticokes did not leave Dorchester County and, according to at least one writer, by degeneration and intermarriage with blacks became entirely extinct in Maryland about 1840. Others remained at the reservation at Broad Creek in the villages of Mattapenen and Nanduge.

In 1852, a small group of Nanticokes from Canada returned to claim 5,000 acres of their reservation, but were turned down by Maryland officials. In the 1890s, the Nanticokes sent another delegation from Canada to Maryland to trace members of their tribe, but none were found.

By 1922, the main body of the Nanticokes was living in Ontario Province in Canada and had been denationalized by the Iroquois. The Nanticoke language had died. In the same year, however, the few surviving families in Delaware organized the Nanticoke Tribal Association and, until 1936, held a Thanksgiving Day Powwow each year at Oak Orchard. The powwows were resumed in 1977. The Association operates a Nanticoke Indian Center and a separate museum six miles east of Millsboro, Del., that are open all year. The Nause-Waiwash Band of Indians was formed about 1989 in Dorchester County.

The Choptanks

Because of its location, all Indian names applied to the Reservation relate to the two local tribes, the Nanticokes and the Choptanks. Over the years, since the early European settlers themselves, there has been a great deal of confusion about these names, and spellings vary. Almost all modern writers and archaeologists have concluded that the Choptanks and Nanticokes were separate and distinct but neighboring tribes. Controversy still exists, however, and the chief of the Nause-Waiwash Band of Indians has claimed stoutly that the Choptanks were part of the Nanticoke tribe. Since the preponderance of the literature currently keeps them separate, so shall it be in this review.

In either event, there was apparently little if any difference in race and custom between the two. Early documents, for the most part, make the distinction, but many blur their mutual status. Some writers claim that the Nanticoke Indians arrived in the area much earlier than the Choptanks. This is reinforced by the studies of one researcher, who found sufficient variations in their pottery to make general differentiations between the tribes and the later arrival of the Choptanks. It is admitted, however, that not enough samples of Choptank pottery exist for definite conclusions.

Leadership

Along with the Nanticokes, the Choptanks were one of the two tribes of Indians in the Scout Reservation area. Unlike the Nanticoke Tribe, there was no "emperor" (tyac), but there were three co-equal "kings" (werewances) over the three Choptank population groups. These sub-tribes (hereinafter to be called "bands") probably represented the areas of their major towns or villages. The kings/chiefs in the Contact Period (late 1650s) were Ababco, Hatsawap, and Tequissino. In their ignorance of the Indian way of life and manner of governance, the English almost immediately began to confuse the names of these men with their villages and their groups, and in the minds of the whites, the bands became "tribes." They also referred to them as Nanticokes in some documents and separated them in others.

It is possible that the Choptanks came to the Dorchester County area from the Western Shore of Maryland and were related to the Conoy (Piscataway) Indians, who were also an offshoot of the Algonquins. If this is the case, they probably crossed the Chesapeake Bay rather than trekking down the Eastern Shore as had the Nanticokes. In any event, evidence indicates that they arrived here much later than did the Nanticokes. They should, however, not be confused with the Yoacomaco Indians of south Dorchester County who were a communications and trading outpost established by their tribe on the Western Shore.

The Choptanks inhabited the area drained by the Choptank River and were therefore the immediate neighbors, to the west, of the Nanticoke tribe. No one knows for sure how far inland the Choptank Indian area extended, but it could not have been far since the Nause Band of the Nanticokes inhabited the directly southern area of Dorchester County. The Nause also had a village at the mouth of the Nanticoke River on its northern shore and inhabited the Crocheron, Toddville, and Bishop Head area. There is no record of any tribe living on the northern banks of the Choptank River. The closest neighbors living north of the Choptank Indians may well have been the Ozines and the Wicomicoes and were 35 to 40 miles away, living between the Wye and Chester Rivers.

European Contact

Captain John Smith, who first explored the area in 1608, apparently did not explore the Choptank River. It is possible that he missed its mouth because of the then-existing "necks" and islands (since eroded or sunken) which screened it, or due to poor visibility in fog or storms. In any event, Smith tells nothing of the Choptank Indians. The earliest mention of the word by Europeans was in a document of 1540 reporting that one Capt. William Claiborne, a Kent Island trader, was set upon by 200 or 300 Indians at "Choptanck." This was probably the name of one of the Indian towns and a place where the English went to trade.

Thus Choptank (an Algonquin word) as a name for an Indian town, may have preceded the labeling of the river by that name. Indeed, "Soptank" or "Sopetank" was the name of the creek now called Indian Creek, which formed one of the boundaries of Locust Neck, where the last Indian town of the area was situated. Perhaps, then, it was on Indian Creek, formerly spelled "Sopetank" Creek, that the supposed town of Choptank was located. This would have placed it near the present Beach Haven community, on the Choptank River a few miles east of Cambridge.

European settlers arrived in the Choptank area about 1658 and began taking up Indian lands, including "Ricarton," later to become Cambridge, in 1659. All these lands fell within the "reserve" granted to these Indians in 1659 and, by 1669, if the Maryland Assembly had not acted on behalf of the Indians, though somewhat tardily, complete expropriation of all their lands would have been the lot of the Choptanks. After serious complaints by the Choptank Chiefs, Ababco, Hatsawap, and Tequissino, the Maryland Assembly signed a "League of Peace" with them on May 7, 1669, and the Choptank Indian Reservation wasgranted to these chiefs on October 14, 1671.

Reservation and Towns

The Choptank Reservation included some 14,000 acres, expanded to 16,429 in 1721. At the time of the granting of their reservation in 1671, the Choptank Indians inhabited several towns on or near the south shore of the Choptank River. It is likely that the three Indian chiefs Ababco, Hatsawap, and Tequissino, who exercised authority over the Choptank Indians at that time, each had a town of his own. Indeed, the first town, Tranquakin, in the neighborhood of the mouth of Whitehall Creek (above or below it) was called "King Ababco's Town" or "the lower town." A second town, in Locust Neck (probably on Goose Creek) was called the "upper town" and was inhabited from at least 1665 to 1837.

How much older it may have been is unknown. Possibly it was originally called "Choptanck" and existed before 1640. At any rate, it was the last inhabited town of the Choptank/Nanticoke area, the place where the last four Choptanks lived. A third town may have been at what was called Choptank Fort which stood somewhere on the Fort Branch of the headstream of the Warwick River (formerly Secretaries Creek). Possibly under the modern town of Secretary, it was abandoned before 1704. A fourth early Indian settlement seems to have been on Indian Neck, lying on the south side of the Choptank River between Secretary Creek and Goose Neck, and next above Locust Neck.

It is apparent that all the lower part of the Indian reservation, including about half of the total river frontage, was without any Indian towns at all. It would seem that the only town inhabited by the Choptanks by 1719 was Locust Neck Town, whose Indian name was Ama-Namo-quun. This was where the remainder of the tribe "huddled together" toward the end, dwindling in numbers on account of emigration and other reasons, and there they finally died out so far as their residence in Maryland is concerned.

Soon after the reservation had been granted to them, the Choptanks began selling it off in lots to settlers. From 1692 to 1720, most of the reserve had been sold in fourteen separate deals. In 1719, an Indian named Tom Bishop complained to the Maryland Assembly on behalf of the Choptank Indians that the English "encroached greatly upon the lands of his people, so that they are now driven into a small narrow neck called Locust Neck." In 1755, the Choptanks were described as "reduced to a small number, chiefly old, crippled, or sickly."

Many things contributed to the tragic decline of the Choptanks. In the early years, there were encroachments by hostile tribes who lived to the north. At the time of the signing of the treaty of 1669, the Choptanks were menaced by the Delawares (Minquas) who had formed an alliance with the remnants of the Wickamisses. Their principal enemies, however, were the Senecas (Northern Indians) who made prisoners of the Choptanks and carried them off, probably for adoption. In 1683, some fourteen Choptanks were returned to their homes on the intercession of the English, but others seem to have been retained. About this time a daughter of King Ababco was released.

Diseases of the Europeans brought to the Indians inadvertently and to which the Native Americans had little or no resistance probably were the major cause of Choptank deaths. Finally, as their lands dwindled, sustenance became difficult and many doubtless died of malnutrition which also left them more prone to disease. Aside from the "gifts" of the whites of tuberculosis, smallpox, and venereal diseases, chronic alcoholism took its deadly toll.

When their neighbors, the Nanticokes, left for the north in 1744, some of the Choptanks probably left also, but most seem to have stayed. One reason the Choptanks lived on as long as they did in the area was the fur trade. The Native Americans were protected by English traders to preserve the commercial status quo. Even when game became so scarce as to be impossible to trap or hunt, the Choptanks stayed on long past when their neighbors had left, probably because they got along with the settlers much better than did the Nanticokes. They, for instance, had not participated in any numbers in the planned revolt of 1742.

In 1792, William Vans Murray submitted a few ethnological notes and a vocabulary which had been collected at Locust Neck Town to Thomas Jefferson. He stated that the tribe had dwindled to nine persons living in four genuine old wigwams thatched over with cedar bark. They were governed by a queen, Mrs. Mulberry. Winicaco, Chief Ababco's son and their last chief, had died about 75 or 80 years before and his body was kept preserved in a mortuary house. In 1801, Mary Mulberry died and her 20 acres were sold by the state. In 1856, a Maryland act stated that the land set aside in 1799 for the Choptanks "has long since been deserted by them, and the race has become extinct." The land then "lay in an unimproved and dilapidated condition" and was sold. A small remnant was retained by the State and sold to the Dorchester County Board of Education on April 7, 1870 for the use of the public schools.

Correcting the Record

For many years, European and American writers believed that a document known as the Wallam Olum contained the creation legends of the Lenape peoples. An earlier version of the camp history, published in 1996, echoed this view and quoted from the document, also known as the "Red Record." Since that time, academic research since has debunked the Wallam Olum. Interviews with older Lenape and those fluent in the language led to the conclusion by researcher David Oestricher that the "Red Record" was in fact a fake by 19th-century scholar Constantine Rafinesque. The Lenape language that Rafinesque purported to document was in fact a near-wholesale creation, Oestricher reported, including actual Lenape words mixed with other languages and cultural symbols.

The 1950s and 1960s

By the late 1950s, Scouting on the Delmarva Peninsula was booming. There were more than 14,600 Scouts in 603 units in 1958, up from 3,368 Scouts during the war in 1940. By 1961, the number of Scouts had grown to more than 17,000, including Cubs, Scouts and Explorers – about a third of boys who were eligible. By 1970, projections called for more than 30,000 Scouts in the council.

At that time, Scouts wanting to do summer camp locally had only one choice unless they ran their own. That camp, Rodney Scout Reservation, was nearing or at capacity during the summer months as home to half of the council's Scouts and Explorers. In 1958, there were more than 3,200 boys projected to attend. A new camp area, Camp Lenape, had been built for $500,000 in the mid-1950s, but by 1961 officials were saying that the three camps – Pathfinder, Wilderness, and Lenape – had reached "maximum use."

In 1960, 212 troops used campsites that were originally designed to hold 160 troops, and kitchen facilities designed to feed 250 people were serving 700 each week. And year-round use at Rodney was also creating strains, with 37,800 campers camping during the winters from 1956 to 1961 – more than 7,000 people during 1960-61 alone.

Against that backdrop, planning began behind the scenes for another option. Wilmington attorney William Poole led a committee that began work in 1958 on long-term camping plans. In 1961, under Scout Executive Forrest J. Sadler, the Council launched a $1.5 million fundraising campaign – or $12.8 million in 2019 dollars – to both purchase and develop a new reservation site and to build a fourth sub-camp at Rodney and renovate buildings.

The new camp – still without a location or a name – was envisioned to hold between 1,200 and 1,500 campers during the summer, relieving some of the pressure on Rodney. It would have 10 troop campsites and five shelters suitable for winter camping; an administration building, commissary and trading post under one roof; and the usual amenities like a swimming pool, rifle range, shower house, health lodge, chapel, and program areas. Southern Delaware or Maryland would be ideal locations, officials noted, giving Scouts in the southern territory a home camp and providing a different type of experience than Rodney, on the Chesapeake Bay.

In late 1961, the location was settled after a three-year search. The council took options out on 740 acres of land in "one of a few sizeable remote wilderness areas remaining on the Delmarva Peninsula," a local newspaper noted. Key players on the council side were special committee chairman W. Ryder Jones, George B. Fitzgerald and John W. Noble, as well as camping chairman Dr. Walter A. Dew and camp development chairman Walter O. Simon. The options were approved at the November 1961 executive board meeting. The first gift for the capital campaign was from the Symington Wayne Corp., and two years later, the deal was inked and the land owned by the Scouts.

Early plans called for a much more ambitious camp layout than exists today. One newspaper reported that the reservation land would hold five sub-camps, like Rodney's setup. Ken Gerlach's recollection is that the reservation was supposed to be home to both the main Nanticoke camp as well as a Camp Choptank to the south, honoring both local native tribes.

The land purchase didn't come a moment too soon. Forecasts projected that by 1964, there would be 19,300 Scouts on Delmarva – an increase of 75 percent over 1958, when planning for the new camp had initially begun.

The camp began to take shape in 1963 and 1964, including the exploration, mapping, and cutting of trails. Scoutmaster Ken Gerlach of Troop 188 of Cambridge, Md., enlisted his Scouts' help in those tasks, spending many nights camping there before it even opened. He worked closely with Ranger Shep Henry and Jim "Pappy" Clark, the Council's director of camping.

Ray Bertrand, then a member of Troop 258 out of Frankford, Del., recalled attending a Sussex District camporee in 1962 or 1963 as a young Scout. "The roads had been plowed up and the stumps were all piled up at one side," he said. "They didn't have the roof on the trading post yet – they had part of it done – and the administration building was done." A handful of the campsites were cleared, and that's where the Sussex troops stayed.

Year One

The new camp was planned on 1,260 acres, with an opening season of 600 Scouts over six weeks of camp. The swimming pool was a must from the beginning, with $25,000 set aside for construction. Six campsites were open the first year.

The first week of camp in 1965 saw 150 boys registered; the second week, 108 Scouts. The first-year fee was $19 a week – equivalent to $153 today. By the end of the summer, 643 campers had walked the trails.

A dedication ceremony on July 18, 1965, was led by Council camping chairman William Poole and Council president Dorsey Kinnamon, with a crowd of 300-400 people in attendance. The administration building was built with support that included a $25,000 gift from the Roman Catholic Diocese of Wilmington.

A Sussex District troop still operating today was among the first units at camp the first week. Troop 89 of Millsboro had four Mile Swim awardees, and several Scouts earned Swimming and Canoeing merit badges. Among them was Douglas Lasher, son of Hiram and Bertha Lasher, later significant financial supporters of the camp and of Scouting.

Bill Sterling, a member of Crisfield's Troop 134, remembers that first summer well. The troop's Scoutmaster quit about a week prior to camp, sparking the prospect of many disappointed Scouts. Sterling's father, a World War II veteran who had vowed never to sleep in a tent again, stepped up and volunteered to lead the Scouts at camp. Sterling completed Rowing and earned a partial in Canoeing.

One of the first staff members the opening summer was Buck Duncan, an 18-year-old Eagle Scout from Pocomoke who had worked for several years at Rodney. Now president of the Mid-Shore Community Foundation after a career in banking, Duncan recalls that first year as highly primitive. The staff and campers were trailblazers, both literally and figuratively.

"There wasn't anything there except a parking lot, as far as I remember, and that was rustic even in itself," he remembered. As a member of the commissioner's staff in 1965, Duncan helped troops plan their week of program – swimming, boating, working on merit badges.

Communication in camp was simple – military surplus field telephones and a switchboard in the Administration Building. "At the beginning of camp, we would run miles of wire, and at the end of camp, coil it back up," Sterling said.

Some Scouts adapted well to the conditions, carving new campsites out of the woods. Others, Duncan said, did not, and let their unhappiness be known. "We had to create a Scout camp, and that's what we did," he said. "We had a lack of everything. You point to it and we didn't have it."

A photograph in a local newspaper from that first summer captured Scout Steve Ramey, of Troop 381 of Seaford, cooking while supervised by counselor-in-training John Britton. John Britton's brother, Jim, was also on camp staff in the early years. A few years later, in July 1967, Jim Britton was killed in a car accident during the camp season. Staff and campers alike took it very hard. Duncan recalled Britton as a very good friend; if he hadn't been off at military boot camp, he would probably have been riding in the car along with Britton, he recalled.

Opening Campfire

Every Sunday evening during the first camp seasons, as dusk gathered, breech-clout-clad guides with torches passed through every campsite and gathered the Scouts and their leaders into long, silent lines as the last light of day faded. The boys and the adults were led to the reservation campfire circle on the edge of the Marshyhope where, in a semicircle facing the dark water on log seats, they participated in the weekly "get-acquainted" council fire. These all had Native American themes, beginning with a deep and resonant voice coming out of the darkness beyond the unlit firelay intoning an invocation as the fire came to life from the torches of the garbed guides. This was followed by the staff being introduced to the new campers by the program director in lively fashion through skits by each department.

As the fire burned down to embers and the program quieted, Shep Henry strolled into the glow of the fire, chewing a wad of tobacco, and adjusted his battered Ranger cap as his faithful old black retriever, "Rip," sat by his side.

As part of his general introduction to the camp itself and how to care for it, he told a tale based on an ancient Native American legend of the area. In the time before the coming of the white man, it went, the Nanticokes lived alone and peacefully on the land, hunting and gathering. The Devil (Ankara) came among them, causing all manner of evils. Game wasn't to be found, crops failed, and there was dissension among the people leading to theft and even violence.

Finally, the chief of chiefs, Malahorn, challenged the Devil to a fight to the finish. They met at the place now called Red Banks and did battle hand-to-hand, during which they fought in the Marshyhope itself. So terrific was the struggle that the bottom of the creek was gouged out and the mud and dirt thrown up into a great mound beside them, forming the present bluff. In the end, the epic hero Malahorn prevailed, hurling the Evil One into the great pit formed there. To this day, the Marshyhope is said to be at its deepest in that spot.

Sterling recalls the campfires more practically. "We tried to shoot flaming arrows into the pyre, but it wouldn't light. We carried flares and tossed them on the pyre; it wouldn't light. We finally got it lit, and cut the dramatics."

Growing and Thriving

The camp's longest-serving staff member, John Dulis, recalled another of Henry's tales, involving the campsite Sandah. According to this story, the depression in the center of the site used to be a root cellar for an old homesteader's cabin where a couple eked out a living. When the wife died, her husband laid her body out in the living room. A panther came sniffing around and began mauling the body, and the widower attacked the animal with a knife. Both the panther and the man died from their injuries, and it took a few months before anyone found the bodies in this remote area. "They didn't bother to try to clean it up or anything – they just set fire to the cabin," Dulis said, adding with a chuckle: "That's one of Shep Henry's stories; whether it's true or not, I don't know."

By 1966, summer camp attendance was projected to be 1,000 campers, with 10 campsites planned to be open along with a new health lodge when camp opened on July 3. That same year saw the first of a handful of lost Scouts over its history – Willis A. Matson III of Cambridge. He was found safe and sound after 12–hour search involving 200 people. Sterling said there were theories that Matson had been kidnapped by spies, as his father worked at a military installation.

Charlie Shaeff joined the staff in 1968 as assistant aquatics director in charge of the waterfront – his first experience with running a boating program on tidal waters. "The challenge of boating on the Marshyhope taught me perseverance," he recalled. But his first memory is of pulling into the parking lot "and being attacked by hordes of deer flies and sheep flies!"

Dulis recalled coming to camp during his first year as assistant Scoutmaster with Laurel's Troop 90, for an Indian Lore camporee in the fall of 1969. "We took first place," he remembered. The troop went to summer camp at Nanticoke in 1971, did its own thing for a few years, returned in 1974, and has been back most summers since.

"It was primitive," Dulis said. "The activity field was all trees at the time. You couldn't get to the rifle range unless you went out past Algonquin."

One day in June 1969, staff members gathered in the Longhouse for a special moment – not to do with camp, but something far beyond the planet under their feet.

"We were in the Longhouse," Sterling remembered. "It did not have windows, just screens. It was pouring down rain, with lots of thunder and lightning. We were huddled around a table with a black and white TV, put together by many TV parts, and spread on the table, watching the moon landing. It was fuzzy, jerky, and dull black and white, but it was wonderful. We were a part of history."

The 1970s

The 1970s saw continued expansion. Members of the Air Force Reserve helped build a 12x24 shelter area, using camp setup and maintenance as a training exercise – also painting buildings and picnic tables, moving tent platforms and clearing trees and brush. By 1975, a camp session was $41 a week, worth $193 today.

In 1972, tragedy struck the camp. Summer staff member Christopher R. Henry, son of Ranger Shep Henry, was found dead in the swimming pool. An Eagle Scout and member of the Order of the Arrow, he was a freshman at North Dorchester High School. He was laid to rest at Old Trinity Cemetery, at Church Creek, Md.

The 1970s also saw staffing changes, at the Council and the camp levels. Scout Executive M.R. Disborough, who had overseen the opening of the camp, retired in 1976 after serving since 1964. The most notable change at the camp was the departure of Henry, who retired in 1979. He was presented with a brass cuspidor – used for spitting tobacco – at a dinner in his honor.

Hired to replace Henry was new Ranger Bill Cantara, who had worked at Rodney for 10 years. Ray Bertrand, an adult leader at the time, said Cantara had a sense of panache. "He used to wander around in his buckskin outfit, which was really sharp," he said. Ray Teat, who succeeded Cantara in the 1980s, recalled him as a grizzled but kind-hearted vet: "Chain-smoked Camels, drank gallons of coffee, cussed up a storm, but would stop the truck to move a turtle out of the road."

Kevin Les Callette, who worked on staff alongside Cantara for several summers, said the two spent a lot of time together. "He had a racecar with some of the guys in Sharptown, and he'd take us over to the Delmar dragway every once in a while," he said. "He was very direct – you knew where you stood with him. But he would bend over backwards to help make you successful as a staff member. And Doris, his wife, was just a sweetheart."

During the summer, the program continued apace – there were greased-watermelon contests in the pool, rope bridges built in Pioneering, canoes swamped at the waterfront and flaming arrows shot over the Marshyhope Creek at campfires by the Order of the Arrow.

Still, the camp was largely undeveloped several years after its founding. Ray Appler, a longtime volunteer on the council, regional and national levels, recalled taking Troop 190 of Easton to the then-Nanticoke Scout Reservation for the first time in the mid-1970s, with his son, Herb, among the Scouts. "It was somewhat barren," Appler recalled. "We had a few buildings, but the camp didn't get a lot of financial support initially."

Les Callette similarly remembered a bare-bones camp when he came to Nanticoke for the first time in 1972 as a Scout with Troop 149 out of Salisbury. "There wasn't a lot there," he. "We had the pool, waterfront, nature area – a lot of it was tarps." Campers signed up for merit badges upon arrival on Sundays, rather than registering in advance. "If there was room, there was room; if there wasn't, you picked something else," he said.

Les Callette joined the camp staff in 1978 as a campcraft instructor and became commissary director in 1981, working with business manager Joanne Stephens. Campers would pick up food for each meal in crates from the commissary, and then do patrol or troop cooking in their campsites.

One night a week, the staff cooked a giant chicken barbeque – though not on Sundays as is now traditional. As there was no Big Top or dining hall at the time, staff would cook the chicken and then deliver it to the campsites. "We'd take it around on a wagon, and a staff member or two would jump off at each site and would eat with the troops," Les Callette said.

The staff in that time wasn't large, he remembered. "Everybody needed to pitch in and do everything that needed to be done. For setup and takedown, we had OA work weekends and things, but it was that staff of 20-25 people that managed the camp."

Rick Meinersmann, then a Scout with Troop 90 of Laurel, Del., was a camper in 1967-68 and worked on staff in 1969-70. His first year he worked in the commissary, Nature, and Scoutcraft areas, and his second in Nature and Scoutcraft.

"I spent a lot of time at the Nature area," recalled Meinersmann, now a research microbiologist with the U.S. Department of Agriculture. "I got pretty good at identifying trees. Sassafras is rare where I live now; I remember it being quite common there, and everybody would get a chance to taste it."

John Dulis remembered one weekend campout when the weather had other plans for his troop. "It had started raining around noon on Friday. We went out and we set up in Toquanni – it was under water. We spent the night, eight of us in the single seat of my pickup truck. It rained all Friday night, it rained all day Saturday, it rained Saturday night – so we spent another night in the pickup. We got home Sunday, hung the tents up to dry, and by the time we got them hung it quit raining, about 2 o'clock Sunday."

Charlie Shaeff, who was on staff in the 1960s and again in 1975-76, recalled how the staff was on alert during bad weather. "The water tower was (and probably still is) the highest point for many miles around," he said. "Every time there was a big thunderstorm, it was likely that lightning would strike the tower with a sound like a big, deep gong! We would then rush out from the staff lounge where we had taken shelter and reset the breakers so the water pump would work again."

Otayachgo

The Otayachgo program ran from 1965 until the mid-1970s, a special program of challenging activities for campers during their spare time. Otayachgo, a Mohegan word for the Nanticoke tribe, also meant "bridge builders," and was chosen because of its symbolism of building a bridge to adulthood.

Upon entering camp, each leader was given enough folded scoreboards for each of their Scouts. The front page featured a picture of a pioneering-type bridge between two shores and a feathered war lance, and featured the words "Otayachgo Patrol/The Bridge Builder." The inside right-hand page featured the following message:

> If you can do eight of the things on the next page, you can be a member of the Otayachgo. If your whole Patrol can do five of them together, your whole patrol will become an Otayachgo Patrol. Each thing you pass must be signed by a staff member, who will give you the appropriate color ribbon to be worn over the button of the right pocket of your shirt.

When you or your patrol have qualified, present this scoreboard to your staff Commissioner. NOTE: Only a natural Patrol of at least five members will be recognized.

The facing page listed the required accomplishments and the color of ribbon (actually yarn) for each. At the bottom were places and dates for the signatures of the unit leader and the commissioner when it had been accomplished.

The award, given out at the end of the week at the final campfire, was a used swimming tag sprayed with white paint, and with a hand-painted Otayachgo emblem. The design had been developed by the staff "artist," a grizzled old veteran from England (and British Scouting) nicknamed "Kruger" after the general who opposed Baden-Powell at the siege of Mafeking, and a real character in his own right.

The awards were produced each week on a production line basis by many staff members. The various colors of yarn were given to each department head, who cut them to the right length for presentation at individual activities. A short length of each color was also glued to the bottom of each award, giving it the appearance of a small Indian shield. Also glued to the top back was a loop of yarn by which to hang it on the pocket button. An Otayachgo flag mirroring this design has hung in the camp's administration building for decades.

Activities included a heaving bar, conservation project, outpost camp, conservation project, swimming, orienteering, rifle range, hiking two trails, flint and steel, knot-tying and pioneering (added in 1966).

Records kept by Ken Gerlach documented the number of Scouts completing each task during 1965 and 1966, serving as an interesting chronicle of Scouts' interests:

Jungle Trail: 292	Heaving Bar: 148
Outpost Camp: 246	Advancement: 124
Conservation Project: 228	Swimming: 108
Orienteering: 228	Rifle Range: 92
Hiking Two Trails: 227	Flint & Steel: 33
Knot-Tying: 224	Pioneering: 32

As seen in the list, the biggest attraction for the first two years was the Jungle Trail, a challenge which also required a certain amount of fortitude, fearlessness, daring, and predilection for getting dirty. Required attire was a pair of swim trunks and optional sneakers. The Trail completed a circuit, arriving back at the starting point, and literally "dropped off" into the wooded swamp immediately south of the Small Homony campsite, traversing about 100 yards of pure muck about waist-deep to a 12-year-old. It involved climbing over deadfalls, roots, climbing a slippery leaning tree trunk, and swinging on a rope into the mud.

Buck Duncan helped create the Jungle Trail as a staff member in 1965. "It really wasn't a trail – just a great big muddy walk," he said. "The Scouts loved it, as you might well imagine."

The Scouts, who were required to be accompanied by a troop adult leader (the guys who really suffered) and a supervising staff member (the younger members of whom loved it), emerged gloriously dirty before jogging to the waterfront for a cleansing dip. The Jungle Trail was dropped at the end of 1966 after a Scout was injured. Nearly a thousand Scouts had gone through it safely by that point.

Shep Henry

No person is more identified with the early years of camp than Shep Henry. He served as ranger for the 14-year period from 1965 until 1979, steering the camp through its formative years.

A Life Scout and member of Troop 2 in Cambridge, Henry would serve in a variety of roles, including Scoutmaster, district member-at-large, and on the council camping committee and his local district program and activities committee. He was a Vigil Honor member of the Order of the Arrow, and was given the Silver Beaver Award for his dedicated service and commitment to Scouting in 1984.

Henry "had more common sense than people could ever imagine," recalled Buck Duncan, a camp commissioner from 1965-67. "He was street-smart. He knew the woods and the territory and the people like the back of his hand. He was a very well-respected, hard-working guy."

As a staffer, Rick Meinersmann looked up to Henry, like many younger staff members. "I would volunteer to do the trash run on Saturdays so that I could spend time with him," Meinersmann said.

Bill Sterling, a camper and staffer in the 1960s, recalled Henry as a great mentor. He recounted how Henry was integral to stopping a nasty habit:

He chewed Red Man tobacco, and I pestered him to give me a plug. I had never chewed and wanted to try it. He relinquished and one day, riding with him in the stake truck, he let me try some with a very strong and pointed warning as only an ex-Navy Seabee could give, about not throwing up. About three seconds of chewing, and I was green and sick. He did stop the truck for me. That was my first, last, and only time.

Longtime staff member Jeff Faust remembered Henry visiting camp in the early 1990s. "Certain people, when they came to camp, there was a reverence about their visit, and Shep was one of them, without a doubt," he said.

After retirement, Shep and his wife, Elizabeth, lived in a home between the camp and Galestown. The couple owned a series of Chesapeake retrievers, all named Molly. "Miss Elizabeth was widely known for her sugar cookie recipe … and other fantastic cooking abilities," Teat recalled, noting that his wife, Regina, still uses that recipe. "Shep was a major prankster and was always getting the best of the liar's club at the garage in Sharptown."

Advice to New Scouts, Scouters, or Staff

"Get outside of the known camp. It makes me sad to think every year a couple thousand people go through there and they've never made it to Old Bucket, never made it to the savannah. Going beyond Ababco and going down the bluff and seeing where Ankara and Malahorn fought – those are just some special memories. … Enjoy every acre of that property. Find yourself without a cell phone, find yourself in a calm mindset, and just let yourself be. Listen to the wind and be joyful."

LEE MURDOCH

"Mind the mosquitoes."

ROGER MAKI

"Mosquitoes are your friends."

CLIFFORD ALPERT

"Just take the time to observe and enjoy the naturalness. … Also, bring lots of insect repellent and boots."

DON COLBURN

"Take advantage of all the programming available. Don't sit around camp, get out and get some training or volunteer to teach or help teach something. Passing on your knowledge and helping people to have a positive journey through Scouting is one of the best feelings you can have."

AARON FURMAN

"Cherish every moment."

CHANDLER SICKMUND

"Make the most of your time and don't just do things that you are comfortable with."

FRANCIS BOECKER

"Go everywhere. Take all the trails."

SETH BRAUNSTEIN

"Walk around the camp. There is so much more to explore outside of the main camp. Lots of trails, history, and genuine Scouting activity."

CHRIS ARBEENE

"Invest in a decent vacuum cleaner because you will get sand everywhere."
AIDEN O'CONNOR

"Take your time and observe it all."

RAY BERTRAND

"Tempus fugit."

HENRY CLIFFORD

"Find what you like and run with it. There are a lot of things you can do at camp and they're all pretty fun, but if you really give it a chance you're going to find something you really enjoy and that will make a difference."
SCOTT CHEESMAN

"Earn the Trailblazer. I had hiked the camp many times. In 1998, David Harris and I took a week in the summer and hiked every trail in camp. It was truly a wonderful way to experience the camp, even as a seasoned Henson veteran."

GENE STERLING

"Take a canoe or kayak out before sundown!"
CHRISTOPHER CULLEN

"The real world will come knocking soon enough, so just do this as long as you can."

ERIC SALSER, AS TOLD TO HENRY CLIFFORD

"As with all things having to do with Scouting, 'Be Prepared.' Ask around among those who have been there before and try to bring what you will need, but be prepared to be flexible."

CHARLIE SHAEFF

"Enjoy. The place is full of adventure."

PAT LENZ

"The property isn't as big as you think it is, and the woods aren't as scary as they seem. Take some muck boots or hip waders – and just get out there and see as much of it as you can. I worked there for years before I even bothered to explore the trail system, and that ended up being some of my favorite memories."

KEVIN STERLING

"Have fun, and work to your Eagle."

JAMES BARBER

"Learn the area, and have fun. Put down the electronics, learn to play poker or chess or even just find a stick and pretend it's a lightsaber and go whack the other patrol!"

ADAM BROOKS

"Make sure to utilize the facilities and give the kids the opportunity to become a part of the program areas and to enjoy the camp itself."

RAY APPLER

"Never stop, but know when to slow down. Explore as much as you can. Be kind, always. Be open minded but not mendable to anything. Be responsible and have fun. Find the hidden and forgotten locations of camp! One day I'll be back and they'd better be clear!"

ANDREW SOLOMON

Your boys will like their hiking. But the experience
they look forward to the most, from the day
they become Scouts, is – camp.

Camp – there's a word that's filled with adventure
to every real boy! It stands for freedom, fun
and adventure!

WILLIAM "GREEN BAR BILL" HILLCOURT
HANDBOOK FOR PATROL LEADERS, 1950

Part Two: Places

The Trails

The Nanticoke trail system is a highlight of the camp, though little explored by most campers or visitors. The original trail map was developed by Ken Gerlach in 1965, but it has been maintained and updated over the years as new buildings and campsites have been added. Most of the work on the trail map has been done by volunteers with the local hunt club, who schedule work days to maintain and map the trails.

Ababco
Orange and White trail; also the name of an outpost camp
Alternate spellings: Abapco, Abaco, Babcoe, Abanvo

Ababco was one of the chiefs, or werewances, of the Choptank Indians when the earliest white settlers arrived. He and his people lived in the area extending from Sandy Hill Point (west of Cambridge) to El Don (currently Bonnie Brook) including present-day Cambridge, the land for which the English paid 40 matchcoats to the Indians. The name of their "king" soon began to be used by the settlers to indicate the band of people that he led and even his village ("King Ababco's Town"). When the whites arrived, the population probably numbered about 1,600 people.

Chief Ababco and fellow Choptank chiefs Hatsawap and Tequissino signed the first treaty with the Europeans, and in 1671 signed the act granting the Choptank Reservation. In 1676, Chief Ababco acted as a mediator between the English and the Nanticoke leader Unnacokasimmon. In 1681, he was asked to join in a war on the English by the Nanticoke chief, or tyac, an offer which he declined.

Ankara
Black & White trail

The Ankara trail was named for the Nanticoke spirit of evil, who took the form of a beast, according to oral tradition and the recollections of Ken Gerlach, who gathered legends from the Galestown/Sharptown area. Ankara was said to be the adversary of the great tyac Malahorn and the heroes Sandah, Singaree, and Toquanni.

A tale told by Ranger Shep Henry at opening campfires described the titanic struggle between Ankara and Malahorn in the Marshyhope Creek; the sand thrown up from their battle created the cliffs known as Red Banks, according to this story.

The trail also formed a major part of the trek called "The Devil's Trail," which was a feature of a special survival program of Troop 188, the first troop to camp overnight at Nanticoke soon after the purchase of its land by the Council.

Hatsawap
Blue & White trail
Alternate spellings: Hatsawapp, Hatswamp, Hatswampe, Ahatchwhoop, Haxd Swamp, and Hatch Swamp

The Hatsawap were a band of Indians living in the area above the Warwick River (formerly Secretaries Creek) and derived their name from the "king" (werewance) who led them when the first settlers came into the Dorset area. Hatsawap was a coequal of the other two chiefs at the time, Ababco and Tequissino. He signed, along with them, the act which established the Choptank Indian Reservation. In a deed of 1726, the Hatsawap and the Ababco were called the "Two Nations."

Noockyousk and Patchyouske were mentioned in a document of 1704 as "rulers" of the Hatsawap. The latter (also spelled Patch Youske) was king (chief) until around 1722, when his daughter and heir Pemetasusk (Pemeta Susk, Permeta Sicsh, Permeta Sisk) became queen and "ruled" at least to 1727. By this time, all the Choptank bands had been decimated in the manner described elsewhere and the Hatsawap were merely a number of the few Native Americans still hanging on in the reservation. Finally, the Hatsawap, as a separate group, were absorbed into the general population remnant.

Kuskarawa

Green & White trail; also an outpost camp

Alternate spellings: Kuskarawaok, Kuskaranaocke, Cuskarwawaok

This was Captain John Smith's original name for "Nanticoke." It appeared as such on his map of 1608 as his name for the river and for the Native Americans who lived there.

Tequissino

Red & White trail

Alternate spellings: Tequassino, Tequasimo, Tequassine.

The Tequissino were a band of the Choptank Indians living in an area on the Choptank River extending from White Hall Creek to the Warwick River (formerly Secretaries Creek). Thus they lived between the Ababco and the Hatsawap. Their land included Oystershell Point, which was built up by the Tequissino over their many years as highly successful watermen. Tequissino was the name of their chief or werewance ("king") when the first European colonists arrived in the area. Along with his brother chiefs, he "made his mark" on many treaties, beginning with the one in 1659. In 1676 he and these chiefs were asked by the colonists to act as mediators between them and Unnacokasimmon, tyac of the Nanticokes, in a situation that might have otherwise led to bloodshed.

Even though some old documents refer to Chief Tequissino as a "Nanticoke," this was not true, although in 1681 he claimed to have kindred "at Nanticoke." In 1693 Chief Tequissino, along with Netaughwoughton of the Ababcoes, was consulted by the English as to the election of an "emperor" of the Nanticokes. In the same year, along with the other Choptank chiefs and the Nanticoke tyac, Tequissino signed a new peace treaty with the colonists. The habit of taking English names appeared early among the Choptanks, and a son of Tequissino was known as "Robin Hood."

Chief Tequissino apparently lived until the first years of the 18th century, for documents of August 1704 and March 1709 name Patasuske to be the "ruler." By this time the band had been living for many years on the reservation assigned to them by the Europeans and had gone into steep decline. Evidence of this is the increasing blending of the population and the blurring of band lines in the documents of the English as the Choptanks found themselves in ever-shrinking limits. The last mention of the Tequissino band as a separate people was in a deed of 1722.

The Campsites

Each campsite features a name related to the Native American tribes, leaders, or history. In 1996, several new campsites were added – not carved out of the woods, but by splitting several large sites in half. Tiawco became Tiawco and Tranquakin; Tamaran became Tamaran and Puckamee.

Algonquin

The Algonquin were one of the great "umbrella" cultures of the mid- and southern East Coast to which the Nanticokes and Choptanks were related by language. They dominated most of the lands east of the Mississippi. As determined by their language group, the Algonquin included tribes, small and great, from New England, Labrador, the central United States, the Plains Country, and west, including two small West Coast tribes.

While most names on the camp property were given by Ken Gerlach, Algonquin was bestowed by Ranger Shep Henry. The campsite bearing the name was originally to have been Sahdow, chief of the Wiwash when John Smith arrived in 1608. Upon seeing the list of prepared names before the first camp season, Henry felt that at least one campsite should be given this proudest of Native American names.

Ashquash

Ashquash was the third emperor (tyac) of the Nanticokes after the arrival of the Europeans. A son of the first tyac, Unnacokasimmon, he was chosen in 1692 by his people after the death of Ahoperoon, but was first rejected by the Maryland government, being declared "an enemy of the Province." After the treaty "granting" the reservation to the Nanticokes, Ashquash was finally reinstated as tyac after a change of heart toward the English.

In 1705 he, along with the chiefs of the Choptank Indians, signed articles of peace with the Europeans. The treaty required Asquash to pay four arrows and two bows annually as tribute; fence in his peoples' cornfields at least seven or eight logs high; and come to any European plantation only unarmed and calling out 300 paces in advance. In view of the treatment of his people by the whites, Ashquash had yet another change of heart and, in 1712, the embittered chief of chiefs fled north, spending the rest of his days in asylum with the Susquehannocks.

Chicone

One of the two Nanticoke Indian towns named in the Europeans' colonial archives, Chicone was located very near the Nanticoke River in the area between that river and Chicone Creek. In a 1676 account, the town of Chicone is described as "where the Emperor doth or lately did reside," and was, therefore, the capital of the Nanticoke tribe. Its location was in the area west, across Marshyhope Creek, from the present Henson Scout Reservation. The town was shown on John Smith's map of 1608 and was occupied to at least 1758 by which time most of the Nanticokes had left their reservation. This campsite was established in 1996.

Kiowa

The Kiowa were Native Americans who traveled from what is now Montana into the Great Plains in the 1700s. They were a nomadic tribe, linked to the Kiowa-Apache.

Malahorn

In local legend, as recounted by Ranger Shep Henry, Malahorn was the Nanticokes' chief of chiefs, or tyac, who challenged the Devil, Ankara, to a fight to the finish. Malahorn was triumphant, and restored peace and prosperity to the land.

Puckamee

Puckamee was named after one of the two Nanticoke Indian towns mentioned in the colonial Maryland Archives, to the east of Baron Creek. The creek flows into the Nanticoke just to the east of Vienna, Md. The town was abandoned in 1744 as the Nanticoke Indians left on their great mass trek north. The campsite was established in 1996.

Sandah, Singaree and Toquanni are names drawn from local legends, tales, and stories told by longtime residents of the area. Some are undoubtedly fictionalized and highly elaborated, and the original manuscripts upon which they may have been based have been lost to time.

Sandah

Sandah was a young brave of the Nanticokes who was an antagonist of the evil spirit Ankara. He grew up to become a chief (tyac) of his tribe, which places the legend before the coming of the whites.

Singaree

Singaree was one of the great chiefs of the Nanticokes and a forebear of Unnacokasimmon, who was tyac when the settlers arrived. He, too, took on Ankara, according to the tale.

Toquanni

Toquanni was a legendary young brave of the Choptank Indians, probably the band led by Tequissino when the English arrived.

Small Homony

In 1742, Jemmy Smallhomony, a member of the Choptank Indian Hatsawap Band, warned the English of a planned uprising by the Indians. It was a widespread plot, abetted and encouraged by the French, who wished to drive the English from their colonies as much as did the Indians. With the Shawnees, elements of the Nanticokes and a few Choptanks were to rise up and, in one night, massacre the English, including their women and children. To this end, with their own women and children, the Indians moved into the middle of the Pocomoke Swamp, built a longhouse as an armory, and began to collect arms and ammunition. A timely deposition by Smallhomony on June 25, 1742, allowed the settlers to nip the revolt in the bud.

Tamaran

The original reference to this chief of chiefs has not been found, but it is believed that the name was a Nanticoke reference to one of the three great men of the Lenape, all of whom were named Tamanend. The first Tamanend became leader of the Lenape when the tribe was living in a territory centered on the fertile valley of the Yellow River, which may be the modern Yellowstone, northeast of the Great Salt Lake. The second Tamanend was sachem of the Lenape in a time of glory and at the summit of their history, around 1450. Tamanend the Third was the sachem who, in 1682, met with William Penn for the Great Treaty of 1682, and "Tamaran" is probably a corruption of his name.

Tiawco

An alternate name for the Nanticoke tribe.

Tranquakin

This is the name by which the Ababco Indians called themselves. It was one of four towns of the Choptank Indians and was also called "King Ababco's Town." It was part of the friendship treaty of 1659 and was signed by King Talacoughkow (Talacoughquan), another name of Chief Ababco. In a deed dated May 10, 1686, also signed by Chief Ababco (written as Abanvo), he described himself as "king of the native Indians of the Lower Town or Nation of Indians in Choptank River – 'called in my language Transquakines.' " Elsewhere, the town seems to have been called "Tresquegue." It was located between Hurst Creek and White Hall Creek, probably at the mouth of White Hall Creek about three miles east of Cambridge and just southeast across the Choptank River from Chancellor Point. The name survives to this day as the Transquaking River which has its headwaters south of the original town and which empties into Fishing Bay. The campsite was established in 1996.

Winicaco

A son of Ababco, Winicaco was "king" (chief) of the Ababco band after his father's death in 1702. He was also called Onoocknotoone in some documents. Along with Ashquash, last emperor/tyac of the Nanticokes, he signed a treaty of peace with the English in 1705, at which time his name was given as "Winnoughquargo." He was the last chief of the Ababco band and died in 1720, at which time his daughter, Betty Carco, became queen. In 1792, when all of the Choptank Indian lands had been reduced to nine people living at Locust Neck Town, Winicaco's bones were still preserved in their mortuary house.

Wiwash

The Wiwash was a band of the Nanticoke Indians visited in 1608 by John Smith. They were located in the town of Nause located in the south of Dorchester County around Goose Creek in the Straits District (not to be confused with the Goose Creek and Neck in the northern part of the county). The village was located at the mouth of this creek where it empties into the west bank of Fishing Bay and comprised the area including present day Bishop Head, Crocheron, and Toddville. At the time of Captain Smith's visit, their chief was Sahdow, which was to have originally been the name of the Algonquin campsite. The Wiwash Indians have again come together in recent years, with the founding of the Nause-Waiwash Band of Indians in 1989.

The Outposts

Along with its trails, Nanticoke's outpost campsites are its hidden gems – little-known to the majority of the campers who come during the summer, but containing some of the best Scouting memories. The outpost sites are purely primitive, with no amenities – just right for a backpacking shakedown, survival trek, or just a night under the stars.

Ababco

On the southern leg of the Blue & White trail overlooking the Marshyhope Creek. Contains a campfire circle with benches. Ababco was one of the chiefs, or werewances, of the Choptank Indians when the earliest European settlers arrived.

Boundary

Located at the northeast corner of the reservation on the Green & White trail soon after it turns sharply to the left (west) from the northeasterly leg. Named simply because it is very close to the north boundary of the camp.

Crazy Woman

Located on the Blue/Black trails southwest of the Camp Maintenance Building. The outpost is located near the site where a house once stood. Legend has it that the last person to live there was an extremely eccentric woman when the building had become a dilapidated shack.

Dan Beard

Located in mid-north reservation near the junction of the Red and Green trails where the latter comes into the Red from the south. Named after Daniel Carter Beard (1850-1941), a founder of Scouting in the United States. Born in Cincinnati, Ohio, he spent much of his boyhood among the Native Americans there and became an accomplished outdoorsman and tracker and expert in all forms of woodcraft. Among his books are the American Boys' Handy-Book;, the Outdoor Handy Book; Shelters, Shacks and Shanties; American Boys' Book of Camplore and Woodcraft; and Wisdom of the Woods. He was National Scout Commissioner and wrote many sections of the Handbook for Boys.

Hidden Field

Found at the junction of the Black and Blue Trails south of the main camp entrance road. When the trails were originally cut, there was a small rectangular cleared area in the middle of the woods which had been abandoned for some years. While the size could have made it a house-yard, there was no evidence of any structure having been there. It was, however, at the end of an overgrown road.

Kuskarawa

On the Black and White trail just south of the gravel pits below the camp entrance road, the outpost was near the end of a road which passed between the pits. This was the name given by John Smith to the Nanticoke Indian tribe.

Lone Hawk

Located at the extreme southernmost end of the Black and White trail below Red Banks and where the trail turns back north toward camp. This outpost was named for a large hawk which was nesting in the area when the trail was first cut. It was also named for its remoteness, for one does not go far from this site without encountering the waist-deep waters of the savannah woodland which surrounds the southwest end of the reservation, at the confluence of the Marshyhope and the Nanticoke. The only way out is north, on foot!

Lost Mill

Found on the Green and White trail just north of where the Red Trail branches from it to the west. When the trails were cut, there was still a great mound of sawdust there, along with the remains of a shed, indicating that it was a major sawmill when the north camp was clearcut many years before.

Medicine Stick

Located on the northern leg of the Blue and White trail on its northernmost leg. Named for a "magical" wand used by the shamans of some Native American tribes as part of the healing ritual. In the Nanticoke area, it is said to have been made from the sassafras tree. The outpost is located on what was the main Jeep fire trail of the north camp.

Old Bucket

On the Blue and White trail north of the camp entrance road just past the Camp Maintenance Area, on the way into camp. An old road leads north to this outpost, at the end of which was a homestead many years before. When trails were being cut, the site was quite overgrown with third-growth hardwoods, but the outline of a large building was visible – either a house or a barn. In the center of the outpost itself, an old battered galvanized milk pail, crushed and rusted, was found, hence the name. The old bucket actually hung on one of the trees for at least the first two camp seasons.

Patty Cannon

Found at the southernmost part of the Black and White trail between Red Banks and Lone Hawk outpost. Named for, but not in honor of, the infamous criminal who allegedly robbed and murdered wayfarers in her inn. She also allegedly imprisoned freed formerly enslaved men that she had kidnapped and held chained to trees in the area until they were put aboard ships to be resold into slavery in the South.

Three Councils

Located on the Black and White trail where it passes atop the bluff at Red Banks in the southwestern part of the Reservation. Along with Ababco, Three Councils is the only outpost camp directly accessible by canoe. It overlooks the Marshyhope behind the low ridge marking the top of the bluff at Red Banks. Tradition holds that Red Banks was a ceremonial site for the Nanticokes and was used by them for great council fires with the chiefs of other tribes, hence the name "Three Councils."

Tomahawk

Found on the eastern side of the Black and White trail about a third of the way to Red Banks in south camp. This outpost was named after the stone ax used by pre-contact Native American tribes across the country. Many fine stone ax heads have been discovered in the general area and are to be found in private collections as well as in museums. A visit to the Nanticoke Indian Museum near Millsboro, Del., would be an excellent way to view such artifacts. The outpost site is located in what was a clearing where one of the first three structures was erected by Del-Mar-Va Council – a two-holer outhouse! It is at the eastern end of a connecting White Trail, which led to Small Homony.

John Smith: Future outpost

This name was never actually assigned to an outpost camp, although it was on the original list. It should be used when a new outpost is established. Named for Captain John Smith (1580-1631), a military adventurer in wars between the English and the Turks until about 1604. He came to America in 1606 and arrived at Jamestown, Va., where he was on the governing council of the new colony there. As far as known, he was the first European to arrive in the area that is now Camp Nanticoke, in 1608. President of the Jamestown Colony from 1608 to 1609, he returned to England in 1609. He explored the New England coast in 1614 and attempted a second voyage there but was captured by the French in 1615. Returned finally to his home in England, he spent the rest of his life writing books about his adventures and explorations in the New World based on his journals.

The Buildings

Some of the main buildings at camp date back more than 50 years to the founding; others were constructed along the way. Nanticoke was built all at once, with the main camp compact and focused around two central buildings. The designers had the benefit of national BSA engineers and their extensive expertise in camp design. The buildings were mostly stick-built on site by the Hurlock Lumber Company.

The 40,000-gallon water tower was a key element of the camp, constructed by Chicago Bridge and Iron Company. The water system was built with Delrin pipe donated by the DuPont Co., a product that didn't sell for long because of the "complexities of heat welding," Teat recalls. Most of that pipe is still in use today.

Administration Building: Built in 1965, funded by the Catholic Diocese of Wilmington. The first addition took place in 1990, with a closed-in porch, additional office space, and a kitchen expansion. The second, with the construction of the dining hall and a further expansion of the kitchen, took place in 2000.

Swimming Pool: Built in 1965; swimmers today use the original pool. It was plastered and had an addition built in 2000.

South and North Shelters: Built in 1966-67.

Waterfront: Built in 1965; renovated around 1994.

Campfire Circle: Built in 1965.

Maintenance Shop: Built in 1965.

Rifle Range: Built in 1965; completely replaced and expanded in 2009.

Archery Range: Built in 1965.

Longhouse: Built in 1965.

Old Chapel: Built in 1965.

Commissary & Trading Post: Built in 1965; since renovated to add quarters for the Campmasters and First Aid station, as well as an overhaul to the Trading Post.

Nanticoke Lodge: Built in 1978.

Fishing Pond: Built in the late 1980s by a contractor mining gravel and fill to build the Sharptown bridge approach across the Nanticoke River.

Lasher Activities Building: Built in 1989. Volunteers cleared the site and built the foundation, with the structure purchased and installed by Nanticoke Homes.

Comfort Stations: Replacing the old open-air concrete block showers, these shower-and-bathroom combination buildings were constructed in 1999 (north), behind Nanticoke Lodge), and 2000 (south, at the swimming pool). The North Comfort Station was built by volunteers.

Climbing Tower: Built in 2008.

Blacksmithing Area: Built in 2009.

Hershey Chapel: Built in 2009. The chapel recognizes Tom and Beth Hershey of Salisbury for their significant gift in the 2005 capital campaign. The old chapel was replaced because the trail there was often underwater and the area housed a significant mosquito population.

The Most Special Place at Camp

"How can you have only one?"

CHRIS JENSEN

"Hershey Chapel. It's a very peaceful place. It was the right place to build it. Any time I went there and I wanted to be alone, just to have some time, that's where I'd land."

KEVIN LES CALLETTE

"The campfire area. It's where all the magic happened."

SETH BRAUNSTEIN

"Red Banks. I don't know if it's the lore around it or how overgrown it is, but I just loved sitting on top of the sand looking down the 'Hope. I also loved taking Scouts for classes there and kept their attention a little more because of the walk."

MICAH MELTON

"I don't know that I have just one. I always appreciated the serenity of going to the campfire circle. It was always nice to sit there and take in the scenery and reflect on the surroundings. ... When I came back as director, I really appreciated and enjoyed the new Hershey Chapel. It was a very inspiring place. It was always nice to go down there – it wasn't too far out of the way, but it was far enough you could get down there and look across the water."

ERIC SALSER

"Tranquakin is one of my favorite campsites – where I wandered off into the woods and laid on picnic tables to watch clouds. Camp is so busy, filled with high energy and people. But it would be exhausting without quiet moments connecting to the bones of camp, the magic of the property itself. That campsite was one I loved, all pines and just far enough away to mute voices during cleanup. The other place that gets me at camp is a little spot just outside the boatyard where a speck of sunset sun blasted through the brush and trees. Those pauses brought on by the natural beauty of camp were fuel for my spirit at camp."

JILL PRICE

"It's really hard to single out a single place. ... There's probably not an inch of the camp where I don't have some great memory or another. From BS'ing on the porches to sneaking turkey sandwiches from the kitchen to commandeering the fire jeep for emergency missions – a lot of magic!"

KEVIN STERLING

"I don't know how to answer that one. The whole camp – the main camp area, I guess. I can go out there and walk the camp without a light."

JOHN DULIS

"The campfire area by the river. When you need a quiet place, you can go there and listen to the water. But when you need good fellowship, spend many nights by that fire, spending time with great friends, and making awesome memories."

CHRIS ARBEENE

"If you'd asked me before 2017, I would have probably said the fishing hole – now the chapel – or Red Banks, anywhere with water access, or the little bridge on the Blue trail ... But in 2017, I got my family to go to camp with me. My son was independent enough to hang out with my wife for part of the day and run around with me at Brownsea the rest of the day. So the walk that we would do – from the cabin to main camp – which I absolutely hated any other year, was super cool that year. Lochlin would hop in my shoulders and we'd walk around. ... That's where he learned to put his hand over his heart when the flag went up and down, and tie knots, and hang out with the big kids, and that was really special."

SCOTT CHEESMAN

Camping is the simple life reduced to actual practice,
as well as the culmination of the outdoor life.

ERNEST THOMPSON SETON
THE BOOK OF WOODCRAFT, 1912

Part Three: Today

The 1980s

The camp continued attracting Scouts year-round during its third decade. A camporee for Worcester, Wicomico and Somerset county troops attracted about 100 Scouts for a weekend of firebuilding, log-splitting, first aid, map and compass, and knots, volunteer and district activities director Ed Sellers told a local newspaper.

To better serve those weekend campers, the first Campmaster Corps was founded for the 1984-85 season with five crews. Led by corps chief Ray Appler, campmasters present for an initial meeting included John Burt, Mike Lokey, Roland Lyon, Tom McDougall, Andy Parezo, Jim Richardson, Joe Schwartz and Sellers.

"These were people I knew that were active in Scouting basically in the southern area, and the fact that they were willing to do things," Appler said. "Rodney had a campmaster corps for many years and Henson never did."

In 1983, Teat was hired as ranger, with the primary duties of handling maintenance and operations. With Ranger Bill Cantara's health having been on the decline, some facilities were in need of major repairs.

In February 1984, Cantara died at age 62 after about six years on the job at Nanticoke. A 22-year Navy veteran who enlisted in the service during the heat of fighting in World War II, Cantara worked for American Dredging Co. before joining the Del-Mar-Va Council. He was laid to rest at Eastern Shore Veterans Cemetery in Beulah, near Hurlock.

Mark Dyer Sr., who was then a camper at Nanticoke, recalled attending Cantara's funeral. "He was old salt," Dyer said. "Bill was a great guy."

That same year, retired Ranger Shep Henry was recognized for his long service to Scouting, receiving the Silver Beaver Award in the same class as Nanticoke volunteer Tom McDougall.

Facilities were minimal, and all troops did patrol cooking in their own sites. The small staff did double- and triple-duty, with the camp director also teaching woodworking and the ranger helping run the commissary.

But behind the scenes, the camp was not financially viable. In the late 1970s and early 1980s, Ray Appler recalled the camp having difficulty filling up for the summer, and some council leaders had begun talking about closing down Nanticoke. In the summer of 1983, there were only 329 campers the entire season.

A review of the finances showed that both camps, Rodney and Nanticoke, were together running the council a deficit of tens of thousands of dollars, Appler said. "So things were not that good," Appler reflected. "My stand before the board was that we need to increase the quality of our staff, and we need to do things as a camp to make it more desirable. In a matter of a couple of years, we turned it around."

Summer camp in the early 1980s was mainly led by professional Scouters like Bob Steele and Elly Mateo. Steele, camp director in 1983-84, spent 27 years with Scouting, retiring in 2013. Mateo, program director in 1984-85, went on to serve as the council's official in charge of Scouting for those with disabilities.

That model of leadership – pulling staff responsible for fundraising and membership away from their normal duties and placing them in charge of a camp – was not sustainable, Teat noted. His interest and ambition drove him to seek out more responsibility. By 1988, he had been promoted from ranger to resident director, a new role and title that recognized his experience and leadership in program and logistics as well as property management and maintenance.

In the early 1980s, a relationship would form between local Eastern Shore hunters and Camp Nanticoke that would stand the test of time, spanning more than three decades. Local outdoorsman Don Colburn recalled hunting nearby property and stumbling upon some camp buildings – the family cabins, as it turned out. From fellow employees at the Seaford DuPont plant, he learned that it was a Scout camp, and struck up an informal agreement with Cantara. "He replied he did not have authority to grant permission, but he would not forbid me, provided I remove my stand at the conclusion of the season," Colburn recalled. A few years later, the Council would give the local hunters formal permission under the aegis of a newly formed hunting club.

Since that time, the hunt club has invested countless hours and dollars into the camp – primarily the trail system, outposts, and outlying areas rarely explored by summer campers. During the 1990s, they teamed up with the Order of the Arrow to do trail maintenance projects. The hunters were somewhat bemused by the conditions under with the new OA inductees worked, but provided keen guidance and kept the clans from getting lost in the marsh.

"The trails were essentially unusable when we arrived," Colburn said. "We've completed many projects, mainly building the maintenance shed and re-establishing and maintaining over 20 miles of trails."

Teat, Murdoch, and other staffers speak highly of the club and its volunteers' commitment to the camp. Members serve as community ambassadors, keep away trespassers, and play a huge role in trail maintenance and mapping. "They also are a significant customer generating operating revenue in an otherwise pretty quiet time of the business cycle," Teat noted.

Cliff Alpert grew up in Federalsburg, Md., right around the corner from camp. As a member of Troop 137, he camped at Nanticoke during the winters and attended summer camp as well. In 1984, he joined the staff ranks as a CIT and then an aquatics instructor in 1985. More than 20 years later, he came back as a leader, serving as Scoutmaster of Troop 90 in Laurel, Del.

The old trading post held great memories for Alpert, who attended summer camp in 1982-83 and was on staff in 1984-85. "It was very small, had a thin walkway, and there was a glass counter in front of you with items on display. You could pick out items behind the glass and they would grab stuff and sell them," he said. A mixed fountain drink with all types of sodas mixed in the same cup was also very popular.

Mark Dyer Sr., trading post manager in 1984, said the space for the camp store was much smaller than today – and lacked air conditioning. "But it was cooler in there, and it was a desirable location with fountain sodas," he recalled. "I don't want to say it was a cake job, but it wasn't that overbearing."

Around 1984, the open area that now serves as the activity field was cleared, Alpert remembered. Previously, there had just been a wooded area with a trail going back to the rifle and archery ranges. "It was still very rough, and there were warnings to kids not to go back there because of briars and things," Alpert remembered.

The health lodge in the early 1980s was located in Indian River Lodge on the main camp road. Alpert recalled on check-in days having to walk out there in his swimsuit for medical checks, and then walking back to the pool for swim checks. "There was lots of walking," he said with a chuckle.

The staff in the 1980s was fairly small, in the 20-30-person range. "It amazes me when I go and see the amount we accomplished with the small numbers," Alpert said. In 1984, the Longhouse crew included about six young men, including Alpert, Dyer, Jeff and Jerold Dulis, and others. Most staff lived in Alder Lodge and the family cabins.

At campfires, staff members dressed in Native American regalia would wait out on the Marshyhope in a canoe with a drum and a torch. Alpert recalled teaming with Jeff and Jerold Dulis one summer – one drumming, one holding the torch, and one paddling the canoe into shore once the campers were assembled, then coming up to the firelay and bringing the flames to life.

In 1986, the property was renamed from Nanticoke Scout Reservation to Richard A. Henson Scout Reservation, with Nanticoke becoming the name of the camp. Richard A. Henson, an aviator and businessman, was recognized with the Del-Mar-Va Council's distinguished citizen award, an event attended by Chief Scout Executive Ben H. Love. Henson's will contained a $1.5 million endowment for Nanticoke. That money was held in a perpetual endowment at the Community Foundation of the Eastern Shore, with a percentage of earnings earmarked for Henson operations and Eagle Scout college scholarships.

The camp gained a new building in the latter part of the decade. The Nanticoke Activities Building opened in 1989 as home to the nature and handicrafts programs. Dedicated to local business executive John Mervine Sr. of Nanticoke Homes, it would later be named in honor of Hiram and Bertha Lasher, who contributed toward a maintenance endowment.

In 1992, Teat told a reporter about all the changes in camp, including a renovation to the Administration building and the improvements at Nanticoke Lodge to allow physically disabled Scouts to attend camp. He also noted Scouting's values of thrift, and the frugal approach taken at Nanticoke: "Everything that's been done in the last five years has been done for $300,000. We arrange volunteer labor, and try and get as much of the material donated as possible."

The 1990s

The 1990s began with a celebration of the camp's 25th anniversary. An event held July 28 involved a rededication ceremony and display of Nanticoke memorabilia.

That was the first summer at Henson for a young Scout by the name of G. Lee Murdoch, a member of Troop 190. He remembered learning to snorkel at night in the pool, sitting around the campfire circle in Sandah, and the floating dock in the Marshyhope. His older brother, Billy, was on staff that year, and served as tour guide and instructor to the camp's patrol cooking system. "As a member of the troop, he was of course given a hard time by his fellow Scouts," Murdoch recalled.

In 1992, the cost of a week at camp was $125, equal to $236 today. About 5,500 Scouts used the reservation each year, including weekend camping and other programs during the offseason.

Longtime Ranger Shep Henry passed away on Feb. 22, 1993 from heart failure at Nanticoke Memorial Hospital in Seaford. Henry was laid to rest in Old Trinity Cemetery near Church Creek, with his son, Christopher, who had died in 1972. His wife, Elizabeth (Schnoor) Henry, passed in 1999 and is also buried there.

In 1994, Teat was named to the Dorchester County Board of Education by Governor William Donald Schaefer. A former president of his local PTA, he spent one afternoon a week in daughter Kara's classroom.

The late 1990s also saw the camp's second lost scout, with a massive search for Christopher Belknap, 13, of Denton. He was found safe.

Forest management became a prime concern during the decade. More than 900 acres were being managed under a conservation plan by the Maryland Department of Natural Resources. Trees harvested for timber were used to pay for the following year's gypsy moth eradication program, without which the camp might have been hard hit.

Eric Salser, who joined the staff in 1991, remembered being shocked by seeing the areas around Tiawco and leading up to Asquash being nearly "clear-cut," in his recollection. "You could see from the pool down into Tiawco and what would bcome Tranquakin. It was like a desert," he said. "I was used to mountains and woods and all that kind of stuff, and I was like, 'Wow, who would want to camp on a beach? What's up with that?'"

Zadock Cropper recalled being hired as archery instructor in 1992, having never attended summer camp at Henson before, though he had done weekend camping previously during Klondike Derbies and camporees. On one canoeing trip down the Nanticoke that concluded at Henson, he lost his glasses in the depths of the river.

Staff salaries were minimal back then; Cropper said he earned $1,600 his first summer and $1,800 his second. For eight weeks of camp, working six days a week and 10 hours a day, that worked out to an hourly wage of $3.75 to run the entire camp's program. "I was raking in the big bucks," he laughed.

Among staff of a certain era, there is a tale told about a summer night in the early 1990s involving a slingshot and staff members launching fruit into campsites. According to Henry Clifford, then a camper, his troop had left the slingshot behind as a parting gift for staff after using it themselves.

"We got round fruit in the commissary baskets – heads of lettuce and things – and we said, 'These look pretty aerodynamic. Wonder if they might fly,'" Clifford recalled ruefully. "We got out our three-man launcher, like any good middle schoolers would, and we proceeded to salute our friends in Singaree. One shot with that head of lettuce and the tent just went 'Whoopff,' just down. We were so freaked out, but I don't think anything happened as a result."

Rob Kuklewicz, aquatics director in the mid-1990s, recalled the Friday night campfires as a particular highlight because everyone had a role to play. To make sure there was enough light coming from the single floodlight, he and Billy Murdoch were tasked each week with setting up and fueling a portable generator hooked up to a buried power cord. "This one task, although it sounds small, was really important – not because of the light, so much, but because we were part of the experience for all of the campers and helping to make sure their time there was special," Kuklewicz said.

The decade was also remarkable for the stability among the camp staff, with familiar faces and names returning summer after summer. "It was a perfect storm where the camp attendance was growing because the staff was returning, and the staff returning was fueling the growth in camp attendance," recalled Murdoch. "Being able to see the camp start to transform and the need to add facilities and staff created a culture that folks wanted to be a part of. The friendships that were formed also drove the retention of staff up as those folks went off to college and wanted to bring their college friends into the fold of their camp friends."

Camp traditions continued, such as the singing of Kumbayah at the opening campfire and Scout Vespers at the closing one. The latter provided a particularly special centering moment for the staff, Salser recalled. "It was the end of the week, and no matter what had happened during the week, everything just kind of came to a halt. It was just amazing to me always the silence that fell over everything. It's almost as if at that point, everything changed from active, energetic to a kind of solemnity, and a recognition that our time is at an end. Until the next time we do this, it's over."

Ray Teat

Shep Henry may have built the camp, but it was Ray Teat who transformed Nanticoke into Henson and made it the modern, fully-functional operation it is today.

John Raymond Teat III grew up in northern Delaware, near Wilmington. He was a Cub Scout in the late 1960s, and joined Troop 522 of Trinity Presbyterian Church in Wilmington in 1970, going camping at Rodney that summer. On one early, rainy camping trip at Brandywine Creek State Park, he recalled being introduced to "cannibal burgers" by best friend and patrol leader Bobby Clark "because we couldn't get anything more than a smoky fire started!"

He began working on the Rodney Scout Reservation staff in 1976, as trading post clerk, and later served as trading post manager, quartermaster and assistant ranger. He became a part-time, year-round assistant ranger in 1981 while he finished his bachelor's degree, and then worked full-time until 1983 when he was named ranger at Nanticoke.

While at Rodney he worked closely with Ranger Jim Brown, a Narraganset Indian, who Teat credits with teaching him much of what he knows about plumbing and electrical maintenance. "We used to climb the wooden power poles on the camp to string the power lines back up after storms," Teat recalled. "My Indian Vigil name is White Warrior in the Kingdom because we were always arguing about something that I knew how to do better than him. Hire a teenager while they still know everything!"

He pursued his degree in forestry and planned to work in that field after graduating from the University of Maine Orono, but then Scouting intervened in the form of that year-round ranger position at Rodney. He finished up his senior year of college at the University of Delaware and graduated with an agriculture degree.

Teat began working at Nanticoke on a bitterly frigid day in December 1983, the coldest winter on record, he recalled. "The water tower was frozen solid and I couldn't get the heat to work in any buildings the first day except the Ranger house," still home to the Cantaras. "I nearly froze that first night – which was my second-ever visit to Nanticoke."

In September 1982, he attended the wedding of a former Rodney coworker in California and met his colleague's sister, Regina Maffia. "I had met her unofficially a few times in those ensuing years, but she had no interest in me. I had to woo her with my wit and charm," he said. They went on their first date on Halloween 1982, and were engaged on December 31. In 1984, she joined the camp staff as business manager. The two were married on October 6, 1984.

The couple raised their two kids in camp – and as part of the camp's staff. Kara and Ryan Teat grew up playing on the trails, sneaking ice cream in the Trading Post, and having hundreds of older brothers and sisters looking out for them. "It was a terrific opportunity to raise two kids," Teat says today. "To this day, there is no one who Kara has never met, and Ryan is the most thoughtful and caring of others individual I know."

Among his chief memories from that time is that of Ryan's birth – and being paged by the camp director at the hospital while Regina was in labor to please bring back four heads of lettuce.

He had his idiosyncrasies, to be sure. During the 1990s, Teat drank his daily coffee from an ordinary mug, but refused to clean it out, recounted Zadock Cropper. "He thought cleaning the mug would take the flavor out of it, so this thing was a white, normal ceramic mug, and it was just caked with black coffee residue," Cropper said. When one staff member got the gumption to clean Teat's mug one day, "he got an earful," Cropper added. "Ray was mad for days, because his coffee mug was cleaned out."

But Teat also had a dry sense of humor, and even whimsy. Jeff Faust, who served as program director and camp director, tells about one early morning when Teat knocked on the door of Alder Lodge to wake up him and Lee Murdoch: "Get up. We're going fishing." They drove down to the boatyard in a tan camp pickup truck, but no fishing rods were apparent. The boat used for motorboating wasn't tied up at the dock, either. "We get in the pontoon boat, and he says, 'All right, one of you get in,' " Faust recalled. "We said, 'What?' He said, 'Get in the water. The boat's on the bottom of the creek.' "

A thunderstorm the night before had sunk the so-called "Hardy Boys" boat – a simple metal skiff with a motor mounted on the stern.

As Faust recalled between laughs: "The plan was to tie the bow line of the boat – still at the dock – to the back of the pontoon boat, and then Lee or I were going to swim down to the boat and hold it while Ray pulled it up to the top of the water, and once we got it up we'd be able to bail it out while he pulled it downriver.

"To make a long story short, sure as shootin', it worked. If anybody tells you Ray doesn't fish, he does – it's just Ray's fishing is not the type of fishing you're accustomed to."

That wasn't the first of Teat's waterfront hijinks. One summer in the early 1990s, he went boogie-boarding behind the motorboat – dressed in a leisure suit, recalled Eric Salser.

Some people considered Teat a cheapskate for his penny-pinching, budget-watching ways. But that just disguised his focus on spending wisely, said longtime shooting sports director Chris Jensen. If something can be justified as a good investment, he'll buy it. Jensen recalled one year when he was seeking to buy a new electric trap thrower to replace a manual one. "I agonized over the price and quality and sat there and made my presentation for a $400 machine," he said. "Ray looked at me, looked at it, and said, 'That sounds good, but this looks cheap. Remember, I'm the guy who buys Volvos and puts 370,000 miles on them. What do you really want?' I said I wanted this one over here, for $1,500. He said, 'Order it.' And we've been using it ever since."

As a boss, the soft-spoken Teat was a master motivator who inspired decades of staff members to go above and beyond. Multiple staff shared stories with the common theme of not wanting to disappoint him.

One recalled how he got a truck stuck in the sand of Small Homony on the very first day he was eligible to drive camp vehicles. He trudged back up to the office dreading the conversation, but Ray just laughed it off as a lesson learned. "You'll never do that again," he said.

Scott Cheesman remembered the feeling that working for Ray Teat inspired: "Working with Ray is one of the most rewarding things I've ever done. He made me feel so connected to my work and what I was supposed to do that I did not want to let that man down at all. … Any time there was a problem, I wanted to make sure I thought it through before I went in and talked to Ray. … that I had at least seen the problem and tired to come up with the solution for it."

To some, Teat had near-magical abilities to sense everything going on in his camp. "He always was everywhere," recalled Henry Clifford. "If you were even thinking of doing something kind of halfway not with the program, Ray would just appear. He'd be like, 'Heh-heh-heh,' and I'd be like, 'Where'd you come from, man? You just apparated out of thin air.' "

David Machinski, whose volunteer hats have included campmaster, cook, council training chairman, and council commissioner, said Teat works by example to pass his philosophy on to everyone he meets. "He's left his mark on many lives," Machinski said. "No matter how successful he gets, he never seems to be comfortable at just sitting back. ... Winston Churchill said, 'Success is never final,' and that's the way Ray Teat shows by his example what Scouting is all about: 'You can always do better, you can always do more.' "

Lee Murdoch, who Teat mentored over many years, said he owes him a great deal. "There's a lot of Ray with me today," he said. "I'm forever grateful for that fact. So for me, the job was trying to honor that legacy and build upon it."

What impressed Eric Salser, who was program director under Teat and later camp director, was that Teat gave the staff immense responsibility. "He let us do things that I don't know other places or people would have allowed us to do," he said. "I never figured out if that was because we'd earned it, or because he trusted us, or because he never had another choice – it could be a combination of all three," he chuckled. "That was a big lesson. I thought that was one of his greatest strengths, allowing people to take on some important things."

Even when Teat had to fire someone, it was done with calmness and control, Salser said. He recalled one summer when three staff members had to be let go after the fruit-chucking incident. "He called them in, one by one, and gave them an opportunity to tell their story. Then he said, 'I need you to go back to your living quarters, pack up your things, and you need to go home today for the last time.' And that's how they were terminated. He never said you're fired, he never showed how angry he was, he never raised his voice."

In 1991, Teat was featured in a profile in a local newspaper, and waxed philosophical about the job. "It's like having a 1,600-acre toy to play with," he told the reporter, while noting that the average summer day was like "a living hell." He explained:

"I'm always here by 7, and usually don't get out until about 10, 10:30 that night. That's Sunday through Friday, with four hours off on Tuesday and Saturday afternoon and night off. It ends up being 90 hours a week.

"Most of what I do is crisis management," he continued. "It's more difficult at the beginning of camp, when everyone is new. Everyone wants to know how to do their job well, and I'm the only source to explain how things are done."

In 2006, Ray and Regina left their home for the last 23 years, with Ray receiving a promotion to council director of support services – managing all of the council's camps as well as a host of other duties, including information technology, accounting, properties, program, insurance, capital projects, and risk management.

The move was not his idea, he admits. "I had to be convinced to leave," he said. "I thought I was going to stay until retirement." But then-Scout Executive Patrick Sterrett was persuasive, and the move allowed for a more normal lifestyle and long-term financial stability, Teat said. In 2019, Teat was promoted again, to director of special projects, where he is overseeing a $10 million capital campaign to build out Akridge Scout Reservation, the future Cub resident camp near Dover, Del.

Reflecting on his long career in 2019, he said it's all been about the people.

"What is most satisfying is recognizing the impact that personal example and leadership have had on the hundreds of Scouts, staff and adults I've interacted with over the years," he recalled. "I continue to be amazed by people who I interacted with years ago, told something or did something with, who I have no recollection, yet that memory or interaction remains important to them many years later."

The 2000s

The 35th anniversary of camp in 2000 was also a celebration of additional progress. After a years-long fundraising campaign, a new dining hall replaced the "Big Top" tent used for meals, and the swimming pool also saw upgrades. The Lasher family was critical in this effort, contributing $225,000 and helping raise the rest.

Camp attendance had grown by more than 300 percent over the last decade, a local reporter noted, and it now held more than 350 Scouts and leaders each week. By 2004, there were 1,300 campers each summer.

At a time when other camps were closing or being sold, Henson's supporters were taking steps to ensure that it would not join them. The camp's 1,485 acres would become permanently preserved thanks to a conservation easement purchase worth $1.1 million with help from the State of Maryland, the U.S. Fish & Wildlife Service, and The Nature Conservancy. Their efforts helped protect 600 acres of wetlands and 800 acres of forest from future development.

In 2004, as the Council was exploring options for a new Cub Scout resident camp, it seriously considered building out the originally planned Camp Choptank on the Reservation property, said Teat. But distance worked against it. Studies showed that Cub-aged families will typically not travel more than 90 minutes to a camp, and Henson was several hours from the population center of the peninsula. The new Cub resident camp is now being built out in phases at Akridge Scout Reservation, near Dover.

The latter part of the decade saw more change. After 23 years on staff and 20 years as camp director, Teat was promoted to council director of support services in late 2006. Tapped to succeed him as camp director was former program director G. Lee Murdoch, who had worked on staff for 10 years, most recently in 2004 as co-program director.

Scott Cheesman, who was commissioner in the summer of 2006, recalled being taken out to dinner by Teat with other senior staff members at the Red Roost and learning the news. "If Ray left and somebody else came in, I think I'd worry about the transition," he said. "We knew Lee, we trusted Lee, we'd all worked for Lee, and we were excited."

Murdoch got his start on summer staff in 1995 as an aquatics instructor. A two-time Kevin J. Thomas Award honoree, he later worked as commissioner and program director, and went on to earn his bachelor's and master's degrees in parks and recreation management. Murdoch pursued a career in professional Scouting, and in 2019 was named scout executive/CEO for the Conquistador Council in New Mexico.

Murdoch said taking over for Teat meant big shoes to fill, as well as a lot to learn. He remembered one early day at the maintenance shed, inspecting the equipment and supplies he was now in charge of. "I was looking around the shop – I thought by myself – when I heard a voice that said 'Whatever you're thinking, don't do it. Don't move anything.' I turned around, and there's Ray. I said, 'I'm sorry, I thought I was in charge!'" Murdoch chuckled. "He said, 'Yeah, but don't move anything because then I won't know where it is and I won't be able to help you.'"

The weather caused challenges, as it always does. One weekend in 2006, the camp experienced what some called the "Great Flood" – a storm that came in from Saturday to Sunday, flooding half of the campsites and making more than a third unusable. "If you stepped off a tent platform, you'd be in ankle-deep or higher water," Cheesman said. Staff worked nonstop until midnight to relocate six campsites – in front of the swimming pool was known as the Dive Inn, near the parking lot was called the Quad. "We did it, and everybody just kind of got their act together and did half of staff week in a day."

On one cold January day, longtime volunteer and hunt club member Don Colburn was working with Murdoch to clear some fallen trees from trails. The two had gotten the ATV stuck in a frozen-over area, and then got Colburn's four-wheel-drive pickup truck stuck on a rescue attempt. "We were considering getting the tractor when I became determined to free my pickup," Colburn remembered. "Finally, I said to Lee we were doing fine because there was only one tree remaining. I heard this whimper, 'I'm freezing, I just want to go home.' I gave him a pair of hip boots for Christmas."

Colburn himself joined the summer staff for several years beginning in 2007, working with shooting sports, but also teaching personal fitness and golf. "Lee asked if I would volunteer to help during camping season," he said. "I was willing for two weeks, and that grew into about 10 years." He reflected on the experience of working alongside staff members who were mostly in their teens and 20s: "It's been great to know them as young people and teenagers, and then run across them now as adults, as peers."

Jill Price, who joined the staff in 2000 as COPE director and went on to serve as program director, said her first memory of Nanticoke is of arriving at camp the first day of staff week. "Driving into the big parking lot and introducing myself to young staff sitting on the fencepost pointing other staff in the direction of check-in. It was my first intro to camp organization, camp friends passing time while doing their job, and the buzz of a new summer adventure."

As the summer neared in 2009, Murdoch remembered, a snafu with the camp's registration system caused one week to be overbooked – "pretty significantly over capacity, as in we didn't have enough tents to physically make it happen," he said. "At that time, Frank Morris was working on the yurts, and our target timeframe didn't look like it was going to get done in time for Boy Scouts. I had to call a Scoutmaster from Newark and ask if he'd be willing to have his troop stay in the new yurts, and he said yes. Frank was able to finish them for the most part so we could have Troop 603 stay in them, and it was just a great summer."

The 2010s

Shortly into the decade, Murdoch left as camp director to move into a role with the field service staff of the Del-Mar-Va Council, leading district executives and unit service in the southern part of the council territory. "He was in for the long haul, and [later] had to be convinced to move on," Teat recalled.

His replacement as camp director was Shawn Pierce, a Kentuckian known for his deep southern accent and a love of hunting and fishing. Hired as council program director and camp director in 2012 was Eric Salser, a veteran of camp staff a decade earlier.

"It was exciting and different – it had changed so much from the time I had left," said Salser, a who had previously been an aquatics staffer, support services director, shooting sports director, and camp program director. "It was a big adjustment from what I was used to, being a small kind of camp where there was a good chance you probably knew everybody to having 400, 500 people and trying to figure out where everyone was going to sit in the dining hall!

"It was good – it was what you want to see in a business, with the growth or continued enthusiasm for what it is you're trying to do."

In 2012, blacksmithing became a permanent part of the program, offering a new way to sweat on summer days. That same year the ATV program was launched as part of a national effort, with Scouts taught key safety measures before being allowed to explore remote sections of the camp. In 2017, welding became a part of the program.

One of the biggest changes during the decade was with the addition and expansion of technology programs. Beginning in 2015, two yurts became the NanTECHcoke area, able to accommodate computers and other high-tech equipment.

"The technology center is amazing," said 2019 program director Paul DeRepentigny. "This year we've gotten an Oculus Quest VR headset, and we're planning to get at least one more."

Campsites are seeing upgrades, as well. Electrical outlets are being added to all the campsites, with the ability to power fans, charge cell phones, or keep CPAP breathing machines running at night. Wireless Internet access is also being expanded throughout the camp.

"That edge is going to put us way ahead of other camps in terms of youth involvement and attendance," DeRepentigny said.

The last decade saw the camp staff boom, with numbers hovering in the 50s and 60s. There were a lot of familiar faces to kick off the decade, with Murdoch continuing as camp director and longtime volunteer Millie Morris returning as camp services director.

In 2013, Ryan Teat rose up the ranks after several years on aquatics staff to serve as program director. Two years later, he became camp director, a job he has held since. In 2014, Craig Richards became camp ranger, noted for his skills in maintenance as well as cooking large quantities of barbeque chicken.

A 50th-anniversary celebration in 2015 brought many people to camp for a day-long event that included tours, activities, dinner, group photos, a slideshow, and a chance to reconnect with friends and former coworkers and campers.

Thinking of the many changes over the years, staff member Seth Braunstein reflected: "Scoutcraft went from Nanticoke Lodge to the Scoutcraft area, then it's apparently moved again. The dining hall was built. The comfort stations were built. The pool has expanded. Brownsea has a permanent area. There's a new chapel. It's so different, but not so much that I don't recognize the place."

The Future

While we can peek into our crystal balls and try to guess the future of Henson Scout Reservation, Camp Nanticoke, the truth is no one knows for certain. Some Scout councils have sold off or consolidated their camps over the last decade, and Scouting nationally faces legal challenges over abuse cases from decades ago. The conservation easement on most of Nanticoke's land may protect it more than most camps, however – as will the continued quality and strength of its staff and programs. Ray Appler, who led and served on many regional camp inspector crews during his decades as a volunteer, said all his observations and comparisons have led him to one conclusion: "Right now, I would rate Henson as one of the best camps in the country."

Programs are continuing to evolve and expand. At this writing, work is in progress on a building that will house the blacksmithing, metalwork and future glassblowing programs. This 2,000-square-foot structure will be enclosed with roll-up metal doors, and could be used year-round for metal arts programs or lodging.

Over the last 50 years, multiple generations have walked the trails. At present, the third generation of the Teat family is now doing the same, reflects Ryan Teat:

In some ways, I have a perspective on camp and on camp life that is very unique. A lot of folks think of Henson as a second home, but it is literally my only home and where I have lived almost my entire life. I was so fortunate to grow up on the reservation. My wife, Kaitlyn, and I are thrilled at the opportunity to raise our children at camp and share with them all of the great experiences I had as a child.

Our son, Luke, was born on June 4, 2019, and has already spent one summer in camp including visiting the dining hall for meals, campfires, and hiking through the woods. I hope that one day my children will share my passion for providing a "second home" to so many and providing youth with the opportunity to learn and have fun in the great outdoors.

It's perhaps most fitting for the final word to belong to Ray Teat, ever a source of optimism:

> The need of our society for programs that teach and mentor young people of strong character and values has never been greater than today. The ability of Scouting to provide leadership in training young people to be productive members of society is as strong as ever. As our membership grows in future years, so too will the participation in camping at Henson.

Nanticoke Through Your Eyes

"This camp has established its own legend and legacy. Its legend is Nanticoke. Its legacy is family. It beckons generations of campers and staff that have seen to bring their children to the camp to share its legacy. It draws campers and staff from the length of the Delmarva peninsula and becomes a melting pot of majesty of the 'shore' and the best of what it has to offer."

GENE STERLING

"Enjoy it while you have it. Because eventually, unless you're Chris Jensen, there's a time in your life when you're going to have to stop. If you're really lucky, you'll get to come back and do it again. It's long, it's tough, and it's hot, but enjoy it while you have it."

SCOTT CHEESMAN

"It was my first time where I not only worked, but lived away from home. You build that bond of camaraderie and brotherhood with all of the guys you know because you work and live together all the time. Those are the life lessons you take with you and memories you carry and things you never forget."

CHRIS ARBEENE

"Most of the staff is like my second family. Such a great group of caring and kind adults who want to make a positive impact on the lives of the youth we serve. … It's a beautiful place staffed by a great group of scouters. I guarantee that if you come to our camp you will want to come back – that I promise!"

DAVE MACHINSKI

"I've made some of the best friends I still have while working as staff. It's a different kind of person that works at a camp, and it was always the worst part of the summer when we packed it all up and ended the season."

SETH BRAUNSTEIN

"Every summer, I spent time with some of the greatest mentors of my life. Growing up in the turbulent '60s, I am sure that had I not had those five summers on staff, I would have taken a much different course with my life. Many of my memories are difficult to put into words, but they are events and relationships understood only through memories and with others whom I have shared those times with. That's the nature of the Nanticoke experience for everyone who has worked or camped there."

BILL STERLING

"Henson is and was a place where the entire culture was dedicated to the outworking of one another in excellence. From the platform crews that continued to set records for high stacks and heavy carries, to the long hours visiting units in-camp, and staying up to the wee hours scrubbing caked-on cobbler out of Dutch ovens – it was a place where you never felt like you could give more to the camp than what it was giving back to you."

KEVIN STERLING

"The staff here are some of the friendliest and most motivated people in the country, and it's always an honor to work here and work with the people who make this camp amazing."

PAUL DEREPENTIGNY

"Just like us, the camp is an ever-growing and evolving thing. The totem pole by the dining hall is no more. The half-pipe in the activities field is long gone. The skeletal remains of the COPE course and the old climbing tower are now nearly gone ... But I think the biggest changes of all are the people. Not just new people, but the changes in the Scouts as they mature and the sameness of the leaders as they return! ... The biggest change for myself and some good friends I admire is starting our families. I can only hope that when they come of age our boys and girls can all go to camp together and create new memories."

ANDREW SOLOMON

The next best thing to really living in the woods
is talking over such an experience.
A thousand little incidents,
scarcely thought of at the time,
crowd upon my mind, and bring back with them
the feeling of freedom and adventure
so dear to the heart of every boy.

DANIEL CARTER BEARD
THE AMERICAN BOY'S HANDY BOOK, 1882

Part Four:
Programs and People

Camp Directors

The buck stops with the camp director, the person who is ultimately responsible for everything that takes place in camp. The CD is in charge of both the program and the support services functions – everything from running a safe rifle range to making sure the kitchen has enough ground beef on hand for tacos.

"The primary job in that role is to build the team to deliver the experience … to create and reinforce the culture and tradition of the camp of 'Enter to Learn, Go Forth to Serve,' " said Lee Murdoch. "The secondary job is sales and connecting some of the key staff with the experience of marketing and promoting the camp to the units."

In the early years, the camp director was sometimes a professional Scouter, a district executive or field director tapped to do summer program duty. In its second year, the camp was run by Philip L. Chabot, district executive for the Mid-Del District out of Dover.

In 1987, the leadership model changed significantly, when Ray Teat was promoted from ranger – a job he'd held for three years – to resident director. The new role combined both the ranger and summer camp director duties in one position.

In the 2000s, after Teat was promoted to director of support services to oversee all council camps and other operations, the model shifted again. Lee Murdoch was hired as a council program director, with duties including serving as summer camp director and overseeing program functions throughout an assigned area.

Murdoch recalled: "Being the camp director was such a humbling position, because I knew that everything I thought and loved about camp was now in my care, and I was the person tasked with replacing a legend in Ray Teat."

That system has continued to the present day, with other council program directors in charge of Rodney Scout Reservation and Akridge Scout Reservation's summer operations. For physical operations, maintenance, and other matters, Henson now has a resident ranger, and Rodney has a resident property superintendent.

Program Directors

For most of the camp's history, the program director has occupied the No. 2 position in the camp hierarchy. The program director is responsible for "everything that happens in camp," as the saying goes – commissioners' visits, quality instruction, special programs, hiring program staff, off-site treks, campfires and campwide games, and more.

Thirty-five people have held the job over the last 50+ years, with 10 of those returning for two or more years: Paul Brady, Scott Cheesman, Jeff Faust, Elly Mateo, Jill Price, Lee Murdoch, Jim Richardson, Eric Salser, Andrew Solomon, and Ryan Teat. Four program directors – Faust, Murdoch, Salser, and Teat – would go on to serve as camp director.

Cheesman said that all the time spent planning for the summer, if done right, means that a program director has very empty days while camp is in session. "The weird thing is, you get to talk about it for so long, and when it's actually running, you have nothing to do. I went from planning it all to walking around going, 'OK, everybody else gets to do all the things.' "

"I had a lot of freedom – like a ridiculous amount of freedom, and that was awesome," Cheesman said, recalling managing the program budget. "I could do what I wanted with it as long as I justified it. We were willing to spend the money to outfit what we needed."

Murdoch said he tried to help the area directors to become the leaders of the staff and purposefully tried to take a back seat. "At the end of the day, my 'success' in those roles was realizing how great of a team we had and letting them shine," he reflected. "As the years have worn on and my hair has greyed, I know that a lot of those area directors helped make me the manager and leader that I am today and I'm forever grateful for their patience and support."

Zadock Cropper, who was program director in 1994 after two years as archery instructor, said he drew on his experience attending other camps and seeing their operations. "I had no clue what I was doing," he said with a laugh. "My thought was I'm going to continue the programs that people like and steal the ones that work from other camps. ... If someone approached me with something, we'd explore it and see if it's possible and a good idea, then we'd do it. If we needed money, we'd beg Ray for it, and end up making it work with whatever we had."

The move from nature director to program director was a little jarring, said 2019 program director Paul DeRepentigny. "Being nature director was so much more teaching than directing, 90 percent of the time, because we didn't have enough instructors that I could float between classes and watch," he said. "So I felt like I had less control over my area as nature director than I had as program director, because I was able to walk between the areas several times a day."

Eric Salser said he tried to create a real esprit de corps among the staff. "The part that was always fun for me – we kind of thrived on it a little bit – was that we took a lot of pride in what we did, and we always wanted to do it the best, and it was a competition to see who could do it better."

Commissioners

In the BSA model, commissioners are unit-support volunteers who help guide troops, packs and crews with good program and operations practices. They are guides and assistants who help the unit but are not part of it, providing best practices and good counsel.

At summer camp, the commissioner plays a similar role as the unit leaders' liaison with the camp staff. Commissioners visit campsites daily for coffee delivery and campsite inspections, checking in with leaders about problems or issues that may have arisen and then solving them. They also check units in to campsites and check them out, making sure equipment and gear is in good condition.

For some years, commissioners at HSR did triple duty – fulfilling the commissioner role, teaching Scoutcraft merit badges, and running the Brownsea first-year camper program. Veteran Scouters with a free week have often stepped in to help with commissioner duties, with the first "commissioner volunteer" noted in 1975.

Henry Clifford, head commissioner for two years in the 1990s, recalled encountering a cicada killer wasp living in the sand on the rail near Asquash while doing campsite inspections. "It scared the crap out of me every day. I'd go and walk past the thing and was too scared to kill it, so me and this cicada killer did battle for two years."

Lee Murdoch, who became commissioner in 1998, said the job in that era was "part customer service, part area manager, and part instructor." He focused on the customer service elements, and credited his staff with giving him the chance to visit with unit leaders. "Those years then helped me better understand what the customers wanted, which helped prepare me for being the camp director better than any other role."

Scoutcraft

Whether it's been called Campcraft, Scoutcraft, or Outdoor Skills, this is the program area most associated with core Scouting skills – camping, hiking, survival, cooking, pioneering, orienteering, first aid, and more. Staff members are expected to be the in-house experts on firebuilding, knots and lashings, woods tools, and backpacking.

For some time, the Scoutcraft program was run by the commissioner's staff along with the Brownsea program. In the early 1990s, it was located in the Brownsea program area across from the Trading Post; when that area was closed off to allow undergrowth to thrive again, it moved to Nanticoke Lodge, with program taking place indoors and in the area surrounding the building. It now takes place in a clearing near the swimming pool.

Micah Melton, who was an instructor and area director during the 2000s, recalled that the philosophy at one point was to call it Outdoor Skills, not Scoutcraft, because all activities at camp are considered scoutcraft. "I kind of like the more traditional name and used it interchangeably," he said.

Brownsea

Brownsea is Henson's first-year camper program, named after the island where Robert Baden-Powell held the first Scout camp in England. First-year camper programs are designed to help new Scouts with the basic skills they need on their way to First Class, as well as acclimate them to the patrol method. It is not a replacement for troop programs, but supplements them with extra instruction and hands-on coaching in a summer camp environment.

For many years, Brownsea and its predecessor programs were a half-day morning session allowed campers to have afternoons free. In 2002, it became a separate program area, and today, Brownsea is an all-day program that includes both Swimming and Nature merit badges.

The program was launched in about 1990 as part of a national push to support troops on the First Class journey. By the 2000s, Brownsea enrollment was sometimes a full third of the Scouts attending camp, Murdoch said. "If you know that a third of your campers on a weekly basis are going to be in a program area, from a management and leadership standpoint it's foolish not to put some of your best resources there," he said.

By the numbers, Teat said, Brownsea is now the No. 1 area that attracts troops to Henson.

Shooting Sports

Originally called "Field Sports" through the 1980s, the traditional activities of rifle and archery are still one of the major attractions to campers today. Along the way, shotgun and pistol shooting were added, and the rifle range doubled in size.

In the early 1980s, Mark Dyer Sr. recalled, members of Troop 107 from Camden, Del., would go onto the rifle range and retrieve the lead bullets from downrange. They carved out molds from a 1x6 piece of wood and then melted the lead over the campfire to cast their troop numerals and other items. "Cooking lead over open flames would probably be frowned upon these days," Dyer recalled with a chuckle.

Zadock Cropper came on board as archery instructor in 1992, fresh off taking a college archery course and joining the campus archery team. That first year, he recalled, he wanted to create an "action archery" range on a trail in the woods, requiring extra hay bales. "I had to beg for $20 so we could expand," he said.

One year the camp didn't have enough money for new professional paper targets for Cub Scout camp, so Cropper dug through Regina Teat's recycling bins and came up with a ton of old math homework from her job as a teacher. "The kids loved it – 'Sorry kids, we don't have any targets, but you can shoot math homework!', " he said chuckling. "I was a big fan of shooting against blank bales or just paper anyway – then you didn't have to worry about who got a bullseye."

For the last two decades, the program area has been led by Chris Jensen, who brought military and law enforcement experience to the role. He has presided over tremendous growth in the rifle program in particular, with the range size and program capacity doubling in 2009.

In the early 2000s, Jensen recalled, the range's wooden deck was like a trampoline in spots. With Scouts shooting prone, "I didn't want to move too much because of the bounce," he said. After discussions with Murdoch, Jensen thought the plan was to build a second eight-station range beside the current one, and was surprised when the old range was torn down and a completely new larger one built in its place.

"Bob Bramble and Lee sent me a text with a picture of a bonfire out in the middle of the range where they just pushed everything into it and lit it up," he recalled. "They didn't invite me to the party, mind you, but they had to show me what they did."

With the expansion came an increase in expenses as well. "We were shooting probably 15,000 rounds a year" in 2001, Jensen estimated. "Within a couple years, we were in the 30s. Now I keep 150,000 rounds on hand at the beginning of summer camp to take care of summer camp and winter program."

COPE / Climbing

The BSA's Project COPE program launched nationally in the 1980s, and Nanticoke was one of two camps on the East Coast to have this type of high-ropes course now common across the country. COPE, standing for Challenging Outdoor Personal Experience, went beyond ziplines and climbing walls to focus on teambuilding and leadership skills.

Older Scouts bonded as a group during the weeklong program while overcoming such challenges as the Wall, the Vertical Playpen, the Giant's Ladder, and the Meatgrinder. A low-level course for younger Scouts, called COPE I, involved teambuilding exercises without harnesses and helmets. The course was also available on weekends for rent by Scout troops and outside groups such as Upward Bound.

Cliff Alpert, then a Scout from Federalsburg, Md., recalled Troop 137 doing the course one weekend in the mid-1980s. "You rappelled off the old tower on one side, and on the other you could get on the zipline and zipline down a good ways," he said.

The new program was a big draw, Teat said. "Troops came to summer camp because of the COPE offering. ... It was popular in the beginning because it was new and unique. We had a cadre of trained facilitators and were able to use the course for things other than summer camp."

Project COPE was shuttered at Henson in 2008 because participation had dropped and the obstacle known as the Wall was in need of costly upgrades, said Scott Cheesman, program director that year. "The numbers didn't justify doing it," he said. "Instead of fixing the Wall, kind of, and dropping money on a program that wasn't super successful, we could put the money into a climbing wall right out front." Teat also noted the impact of increasing regulation and changes to construction standards that required "expensive re-construction."

There was no high-ropes element during the summer of 2009, but in 2010 a new climbing tower reopened in the activities field at the site of the former COPE storage shed.

Nature & Ecology

The Nature Lodge for many years has been housed at the Lasher Activities Building, near the swimming pool. Inside holds class space, animal exhibits, and educational displays and posters, while nature identification trails and ecology demonstrations are outdoors.

A consistently popular program area, the nature program has evolved over the years in acknowledgement of the fact that not all topics are designed for all Scouts. The modern-day program includes core "nature" merit badges like Nature, Animal Science, Fish and Wildlife, Reptile and Amphibian Study, Mammal Study, and Weather for all Scouts. Recommended for older Scouts are the "ecology" badges of Environmental Science, Insect Study, Forestry, Soil and Water Conservation and Chemistry.

There have always been critters of some sort in the Nature Lodge. For some years, there were noxious hissing cockroaches on display. Paul DeRepentigny recalled one day when a Northern Water Snake got out of her tank and went missing. "We spent half an hour looking everywhere for her until an adult leader opened a random drawer and the snake was coiled up," he said. "Still don't have a clue how she got in there."

Handicrafts

The Handicrafts program area includes the traditional Scouting crafts of woodcarving, leatherwork, and basketry – time-honored skills with ancient roots that can take years to master. It has also at times included Indian Lore, and in recent years has been home to pottery, art, painting and graphic design activities.

Until recent years, Handicrafts lacked a permanent home like other program areas. In the early 1980s, it was located on the end porch of the administration building. In the mid-1990s, it was co-located in the Lasher Activities Building alongside the nature and ecology programs. Squeezing whittling and basket-weaving Scouts into close quarters was not optimal, and it has since moved to a home in the Nanticoke Lodge, providing space for supplies and equipment storage.

Aquatics

At some camps, the aquatics program is focused centrally at the waterfront. Henson's program, by necessity, requires two qualified leaders – one at the pool and one at the Marshyhope Creek to oversee the boating program. Both areas are key attractions for Scouts, whether to learn a new skill or just cool down in the water.

The pool's program for years has included basic instructional swimming; Swimming merit badge; Lifesaving merit badge; and open swimming periods. The pool was expanded in 2000.

Paul DeRepentigny recalled earning Swimming merit badge at age 16 after failing it years prior while taking Brownsea: "None of my dives were good enough to finish the requirement until I basically just launched myself into the pool," he said. "My goggles snapped from how hard I hit the water, and my nose piece came off so water got in my nose and I came up coughing, but the instructor said it was a perfect dive."

In 2000, aquatics instructor Chris Arbeene had a friendly "Bronze God" competition with fellow instructor Rob Malone. Arbeene was stationed at the pool, while Malone was at the waterfront, and that gave him an edge. "We got about three-quarters of the way through the summer, and he was like, 'I give up. You win,'" Arbeene recalled. "I spent hours a day in the pool all summer, from Boy Scouts to Cub Scouts, just teaching swimming and lifeguarding for open swims. I was literally a fish that summer."

The Marshyhope Creek offers Scouts the chance to canoe, kayak, row, sail, or drive a motorboat. Flotillas setting out from the dock to practice the J-stroke or flipping their boats is always a fun sight. The camp has operated a pontoon boat for many years for motorboating; it does double duty at other times as a platform for swimming and fishing. Waterskiing, wakeboarding, and tubing are also key parts of waterfront activities.

Ray Appler, who ran the waterfront for several years, recalled expanding from one leaky runabout to a fleet of sailboats plying the Marshyhope. "People said you couldn't sail on it. I said, 'Yes, you can.' It was a beautiful place to sail," he said. "We're the envy of other camps."

Special Programs

A camp can't thrive by just offering the same programs year after year. The Henson leadership has been particularly inventive in creating new opportunities to attract Scouts, especially older ones. In the 1990s when BMX biking was a craze, the camp had a staffer assigned to run a BMX course. A few years ago, the camp became one of the first Scout camps in the nation to offer both an ATV safety program and a pistol-shooting program. Special fitness offerings, including golf, have joined the mix at times, and Scouts have in some years spent most of the week cycling, paddling and backpacking their way around the Eastern Shore on "ecotour" or similarly-styled adventure treks.

One year, Scouts were taken offsite each day for a new experience – deep-sea diving one day, flying in an airplane the next, recalled Cheesman. A recently launched technology area now includes game design, robotics, digital technology, and drone racing. Visual arts includes moviemaking and photography. And for Scouts who like to work with their hands, there are now metalworking and welding programs.

For three years, from 1988-1990, the camp offered Horsemanship merit badge, thinking it would attract campers. "It turned out to not be so overwhelmingly popular with mostly rural campers," Teat recalled. "It was very expensive to run and even harder to staff well … but it was fun while we did it."

Trail to Eagle / Eagle Base

In an effort to help Scouts along the path toward the Eagle Scout rank, Henson has had an older-Scout program for the last 30 years where specialized merit badges and experiences were offered.

In its earliest incarnation, it was known as the Trail to Eagle camp, taking place during the school holiday from Christmas to New Year's. Later, it ran for a full summer week after the conclusion of the regular camp sessions. The all-volunteer staff taught merit badge subjects like Citizenship in the Nation and Communications – items not traditionally taught at summer camp. Scouts could work at those specialized badges while enjoying the pool, waterfront, and other program areas. Under program director Tom McDougall, Trail to Eagle thrived for several years.

In 1996, it was folded into the main camp sessions under the name Eagle Base, run the first year by staff member Jeff Faust. Scouts could either attend as part of an Eagle Base provisional unit or take merit badge classes while attending with their own troops. Since then, it has usually been run by a staff member and supplemented with volunteer instructors.

Cub Scouts

The Cub Scout resident camp program was launched to offer new outdoor experiences to the Cub population which makes up the largest part of Scouting's youth membership, Teat said.

Cub resident camp generally had a new theme each year that staff would adopt and customize their activities, such as Knights of the Roundtable, Pirates of the Nanticoke, or space. "That made it a lot easier" to come up with program ideas, said Zadock Cropper, program director in 1994. "You have your topic, and then you conform to the topic."

Staff would often wear costumes and take on themed titles. For many years, younger staff played the roles of "Squires" or "First Mates" – program specialists who led Cubs around to different areas, played games, and sang songs. Program areas were heavily decorated, with cardboard or canvas castles, pirate ships, or spaceships and makeshift planetary landing craft. The last day of camp would often end with the World's Largest Ice Cream Sundae – eaten directly with hundreds of plastic spoons from a massive foil-lined raingutter trough.

Cubs could stay for a full week or half-week session. One unique activity for the weeklong campers was an outpost trip to Ababco, where they would spend an afternoon cooking, swimming in the creek, hiking, and doing special activities. Sometimes they would camp there overnight. That provided some variety for campers and staff, and also cleared out the main camp for new half-week units to move in seamlessly.

Cropper remembered giving a safety speech to some Webelos at the outpost, including a stern warning not to touch the abundant prickly pear cactii. "Every other word out of my mouth is 'Never touch. Don't touch it,' " he recalled. "But then I showed them how to peel and actually eat the cactus, and everyone had a little bit. For the rest of the trip, all the kids were trying to pick up the cactus because they didn't quite listen, and we were peeling the pricklers out of everbody's fingers for the rest of the day. It was a good lesson," he added ruefully.

The switch between programs could be mentally jarring for some. "To be great, like my Webelos first aid routine I did one year, you had to customize for Cubs – not only a different program, but different programs for each age group," Micah Melton said. "The designing was challenging, but made Cubs more fun because most of the time they still never got bored being at camp."

During the 1990s, the program was bursting at the seams, with Cub Scout attendance dominating the summer. Today, with a surge in local Cub day camp programming, that has been reduced to two weeks of Cub resident camp. That mirrors the national trend in Cub Scout camping, Teat noted. As a result, the number of Cub camp staff members has also been trimmed; staff members no longer serve as program specialists or guides to dens and troops, DeRepentigny said. "We can run the whole Cub camp with 20 program staff," he said. "It's significantly smaller."

Within the next several years, the plans are for Cub resident camp to leave Henson entirely. The new Akridge Scout Reservation will open as a Cub resident camp, and Henson will have an additional week of Scouts BSA summer camp added.

Nanticoke also has been home to other Cub Scout activities, such as Sussex District's chariot races in the 1980s. Each den would build a wheeled chariot for one Scout to ride in, pulled by the others, and race around the trails to stations such as knot-tying and nail-driving. Cropper wistfully recalled those dashes around the main camp loop: "Those were fun." Adam Brooks of Cambridge remembered his first campout with his father in Cubs, which also involved a Pinewood Derby: "I won one heat, but then my car got jammed."

Kevin Les Callette, who went on to a career in professional Scouting in the Baltimore Area Council and then back home in Del-Mar-Va Council, said one of the things that sets Henson's Cub program apart was the creativity of its staff in developing activities and program areas from scratch out of the woods each summer. "As I traveled around and visited other camps, I'd see they would build these ships and castles and stuff – these monstrous facilities – and then they'd hope people would come and use them. At Henson, it was 'We're going to build it each summer. We don't need any ships – we can make our own ship.' It was just the creativity that was needed, and kids appreciated that more."

Support Services

The term "support services" is vague, but covers a wide range of functions that no camp would operate without. Support services staff often labor behind the scenes, working without recognition or the public thanks that program staff – the public face of the camp – often receive. Staff members cook and serve meals, repair buildings, unclog shower drains, patch tents, provide first aid, answer phones, sell items in the Trading Post, issue sports gear from the commissary, and carry out a host of other thankless duties.

Micah Melton, who worked in the trading post in 2006-07 and would later serve as camp services director, said he learned a lot working on the support services side that helped him in his jobs beyond camp. "I missed working directly with Scouts when I was in services, but I got to see a lot of the hard interworkings of camp," he recalled.

Bill Sterling, who was trading post manager in the late 1960s, said the operation had run a deficit the previous two years when he came on board. He offered special deals to eliminate that – personally sewing moccasins or painting neckerchief slides for Scouts who purchased them. "We eliminated the inventory and turned a profit," he recalled.

Three decades later, his son, Gene, would also run the trading post for a summer. "It always horrified me taking the receipts to Ray, because they were never right. They were always either over or short. I remember telling Ray, 'I don't even know how to make you understand I am not stealing money from the trading post!' " he said. "I think I had one time where it actually cleared, everything was right, but I had circled the wrong number. I just can't win." Nevertheless, he ended up making one key sale – convincing a unit leader to buy the first Dutch oven from the store in years.

Camp Food

Traditional summer camp food has always gotten a bad rap – think great green gobs of greasy grimy gopher guts. That's perhaps expected when dealing with the picky palates of young people. But the food at Henson has always gotten solid praise over the years, with a wide variety of dishes and items to suit many preferences. Opening dinners for many years included roasted pig or BBQ chicken; other meals included tacos, baked potatoes, and sandwiches of many varieties.

"What's the one place in camp that everyone goes to three times a day? The dining hall, right?" said Lee Murdoch, explaining the critical role of an excellent food service team. "I've always thought that if you had bad food, no matter how good your program is, nothing would ever overcome that. If you had good food, everything else is OK. But if you don't have good food, man, it is like you're dead in the water, the sharks are circling, and you're fighting an uphill battle that you're not going to win."

Cooking in campsites was the tradition from 1965 until about 1990. Campers hauled in water in plastic three-gallon jugs and cooked over charcoal stoves in patrols, with food issued from the commissary. Cliff Alpert recalled troops in the early 1980s picking their grub and supplies up at the commissary before each meal and carting it back to their campsites to cook. "You had to go through the inventory list and make sure you doublechecked and had everything. What if you got back to the troop and were missing eggs or what-have-you?"

Getting the food to camp was an adventure, recalled Kevin Les Callette, commissary director for two years in the early 1980s. There were no Sysco tractor-trailers delivering giant boxes and pallets like today. Instead, staffers would have to grab a truck and head to market – purchasing chicken from Perdue Farms, canned goods from a cash-and-carry place in Salisbury, and produce at a market in Mardela Springs.

In the mid-1980s, Nancy Webb joined the staff for a tremendous 11 years as camp chef. "She could COOK," Teat recalled with emphasis. "Lots of butter, sugar, and salt in everything, and her slippery dumplings are unparalleled to this day." Webb and her successors presided over a tight-knit crew that kept longer hours than anyone – their workday began before 5 a.m. and often didn't end until after 9:30 p.m., with very few pauses or opportunities to sit down.

In 1990, the camp introduced "heater stack" cooking. Units would pick up insulated carriers of pre-cooked, heated ingredients at the commissary and cart them back to their campsites, to be assembled into a meal and eaten. Scouts could devour hot scrambled eggs and bacon in the morning without the mess of cooking, and only had to clean up personal dishes.

All-camp meals were only on Sunday and Friday nights for opening and closing, held under the Big Top tent where the dining hall now stands. Staff members hungry after a long day routinely raided the kitchen late at night for peanut butter (or almond butter) and jelly, and were known to sneak into the commissary for snacks like handfuls of pepperoni slices.

By the latter part of the decade, units were eating all meals under the circus tent known as the Big Top, using family-style serving methods, an innovation which freed up program time. It also had become a struggle to prepare meals for an entire camp in a kitchen designed to only feed the camp's staff.

Each night under the giant tent, staff members would assemble to clean off the concrete pad underneath the tent – a rapid-fire process of moving tables off, spraying down the pad, dousing it with a solution of bleach, squeegeing the water off, and moving the tables back. The tent itself had to be monitored during rainstorms for pockets of water that would form near the edges; they had to be carefully pushed up and out to avoid a messy backsplash on those sitting nearby.

In 2000, the Big Top came down for good and a new dining hall opened, part of a $1 million fundraising campaign that included expanding the swimming pool. With attendance having grown by more than 300 percent over the decade, the new building was greatly needed. The dining hall was dedicated to the Lasher family, who contributed $225,000 and helped raise the rest of the funds, and Frank and Millie Morris were singled out for their time and effort. "They put their all into this project," Teat told a local newspaper.

"When I came here 35 years ago as a Scout, it was a great place to come," recalled Dorchester County Chamber of Commerce president Gage Thomas at the dedication event. "It's still great to come back here."

Ray Appler remembered his contribution to the dining hall project – working with Ray Teat to build the tables and benches that are still in use today. "I would build the legs at home, Ray would come with a truck and haul them down to camp. I'd go down to the warehouse, we'd hook up the woodstove and I'd saw and cut and bolt and everything, and it held up."

Still, camp food has come in for some ribbing, as it does anywhere. Scott Cheesman recalled a skit one year that made fun of the menu: "It was an 'SNL' newsroom-type skit, but the highlight was the menu for the week that went something like this: 'Monday, chicken patties; Monday night, baked chicken; Tuesday, chicken nuggets; Wednesday, BBQ chicken.' "

Roast pig was a big hit with campers for many years. The huge pigs were loaded into a cooker and roasted all day long. Henry Clifford remembered being volunteered with another staff member to get up at 4 a.m. and take care of the pig.

"We went into the walk-in, and the pig basically consumed the entire space. We were like, 'What the heck do we do with this thing?' It was like two murderers moving a body, heaving this dead weight onto a cart," Clifford said. "When we finally got it up to the cooker, we were wrestling it and heaving it and we were grunting and cursing and it won't fit. The two legs are hanging out. So we went and got a saw and we had to saw the legs off this pig so it would fit into the cooker.

"We went to bed, and at breakfast, Ray's just like 'Hey, thanks.' We were like, 'Never be around when it's time to put the pig on the cooker.' "

Campmasters

If the summer staffers are the heart of the camp during the summer, then volunteer campmasters are the heart of the camp year-round. The Campmaster Corps formed in 1984 under longtime volunteer Ray Appler, providing a group of committed, dedicated Scouters to keep the camp open on weekends in the fall, winter and spring. Campmasters would check in units, run specialized program offerings, do basic maintenance, and assist units in emergencies.

"All of us are not there for any recognitions," said longtime Campmaster Ray Bertrand. "Our job is to help the Scoutmaster and make sure the Scouts get a decent program."

Shooting sports is the most popular program by far, with some units returning every year for a weekend on the ranges with their favorite campmasters. Current programs include scavenger hunts, railroading, GPS and orienteering, and first aid. Founding chief campmaster Ray Appler still serves at age 84, joining his wife and son on a crew.

Bertrand said one of his favorite experiences is walking the camp in moonlight. "Every night before we settle down, we patrol the camp to make sure fires are down," he explained. "We usually don't carry a flashlight, since we're so used to the roads we know where we're going, and full-moon nights are naturally the best time."

Since 1998, the campmasters have kept a regular log chronicling their adventures and exploits. The hard-bound brown-and-black record book notes the weather, units in camp, programs offered, maintenance issues, and occasionally flashes of humor.

From March 1999, Dulis Crew: "The Nanticoke Lodge needs a sink stopper. Baltimore troop made due using a patrol leader's finger, but we need to get this fixed as he has to leave for school on Wednesday."

From October 2004, Murdoch Crew: "Tried some of the candy and almost got sick (too many Pixie Sticks)."

And in January 2011, an unnamed crew member put part of the weekend to verse:

Cold it started – cold it stayed
The heater kept on going
The best thing about the weather –
It didn't end up snowing!

Edie had no working phone
And the credit card machine was down
But in true Scout Spirit she pressed on
With a smile – not a frown.

Lee Murdoch, who lived at camp year-round during his time as camp director, said the chance to work alongside the campmaster corps members was humbling. "I realized that the camp was a living, breathing thing that was cared for just as deeply by others as it was by me," he said. "That gives me such great pleasure to know that the camp will live on because of its unique ability to capture the spirit of friendship and family, and that will continue to grow for the next generation of campers."

Winter Camping

Some memories are inextricably tied to winter camping. Cliff Alpert recalled a Klondike Derby in the winter of 1986 when a blizzard powered in with thundersnow. "The fire pits were those big tractor-trailer wheels, and we had about four of them stacked up – like a 55-gallon drum – glowing red-hot because it was so cold out," he remembered.

Chris Arbeene recalled his first introduction to Henson was at a 1995 Klondike Derby. "It was frigid cold – the high for Saturday was like 25 degrees, and of course it was windy," he said. "We lashed together our sled and went to the Activity Field to race it."

For 50 years, both Rodney and Nanticoke – and later Akridge – have offered a special winter camping patch, with a distinctive white background and red border and an animal at the center. "The animals selected are indigenous species and alternate from mammal to bird every other year," Teat explained. To mark the anniversary of the program in 2020, the 2019-20 patch is a reprint of the original raccoon patch from 1970.

Still, winter camping doesn't always mean dressing in layers and combating frigid temperatures. John Dulis remembered a few weekends: "We got the frostbite patch, but the two weekends we were in camp we were running around with short sleeves on. It was about 65-70 degrees. You never know what you're going to run into!"

World Scouting

For much of the camp's history, international staff members – Scouts in their home countries – were a common sight along the Marshyhope. They lived and worked alongside the U.S. staff, teaching programs, serving on support staff, and living in tents and cabins. Some were hosted by local Scouting families on their days off. The flags of their countries sometimes flew alongside the Delaware, Maryland and Virginia flags on the main camp flagpole, and were presented to staff members from those countries at the closing flag ceremony on Saturday.

In 1971, Kristian Graversgaard-Knudsen of Denmark, a 27-year-old teacher, made his first trip to the United States on the Nanticoke staff, helping the camp commissioner. A local newspaper reporter paraphrased him: "In both the U.S. and Denmark the scoutmasters come to camp with one idea, that the boys, not the scoutmaster, should have a good camp." Graversgaard-Knudsen worked at Nanticoke from June to mid-August and then did a stint at Rodney before returning home.

A few years later, camp was home to Seiji Sugiura of Japan, helping teach swimming, pioneering and wilderness survival topics on a summer break from college. A reporter noted: "The things he likes best about the Eastern Shore is its seafood. Crabs are a favorite. When asked what seafood was popular in Japan that wasn't served here he mentioned octopus, squid, blow fish and eel." Sugiura's career goal was to return to the U.S. and work as a professional Scouter.

From his home in Japan nearly five decades later, Sugiura recalled his time at Nanticoke with fondness. His first trip to the United States was in 1973 at the National Jamboree in Pennsylvania. He later joined up through the international camp staff program and came to Maryland. "I met wonderful people at Nanticoke," he said. "Every staff was kind and friendly." He remembered one campwide game with the mission of catching staff members wearing a Nanticoke t-shirt and red Scout garters. "Maybe the camp director announced about the game at the morning meeting, but I did not listen," he said. "I was surrounded by many Scouts ... then stripped of my t-shirt and red garters, and they were gone." The staff ended up buying him a new t-shirt.

"All of these guys brought immense good fortune on Nanticoke," Teat recalled, mentioning 1980s-era staff from South Africa, the Netherlands, and Germany. In the early 1990s, one Scout recalled a staff member from the U.K. regaling his troop over lunch with a description of haggis – a national dish consisting of oatmeal in a sheep's stomach.

Steve Walker, a British Scout from Manchester, England, was assigned to the aquatics staff. Unfortunately for him, he burned in the sun and spent most of the summer bright red, recalled Eric Salser. Dolf Groen was shooting sports director in 1992 – a fitting job for a man who was a military sharpshooter in Holland. He also spoke five languages, bringing additional international flavor to rural Maryland.

The staff members helped connect Scouts from Delmarva with a broader world and different cultures, said Salser, who recalled many of his colleagues with fondness. "Whether it was the flags or their uniforms, or the idea that you could meet somebody from a different place – not across the bridge or Philadephia, but you were meeting somebody from a different *place* – how unique that was. … It gave you that sense of what it might like to be in Scotland or to be in Holland. … It was a good experience for the kids – it was a good experience for me! We had a lot of fun and a real great time."

Sugiura reflected: "Once a Scout, always a Scout, B.P. said. … No matter how different skin colors and languages, we are acting under the B.P. spirit towards the same purpose."

Bowling Pins

Bowling pins have been a key part of camp and a unique tradition since the first days. While Henson has never had a bowling alley, used bowling pins managed to turn up over the years and find their way into the hands of Scouts and staffers.

Known in camp parlance as a "schmoo," the humble bowling pin primarily serves as an all-purpose hammer, helping staff during camp set-up with pounding in tarp stakes. Schmoos are also handy for quickly adjusting a tent 4x4 or outrigger, the wide base distributing the force evenly and not splintering the wood. When reversed, the neck fits comfortably into one's hand.

The primary benefit is that they're cheap and easily replaceable. You can toss a schmoo into the back of a truck while on a job, and leave it there for days in the rain and sun. If you were to do that to an ordinary hammer, the ranger would be hunting you down for his tools.

The schmoo tradition dates back to the very first summer. Bill Sterling, a camper in 1965, recalled how his troop got 100 percent on daily campsite inspections that first year. "We were awarded the Schmoo award at the end of the week, which was a bowling pin wrapped in foil," he said.

The name "schmoo" has its origins in the classic Li'l Abner comic strip, with "shmoo" being the name of a race of odd little creatures that resemble bowling pins.

Camp Memories

"Working aquatics staff with Jeff [Dulis] and how hard he made me work on lifesaving escapes my CIT year. Those skills saved my life a few times in the Navy, years later."

AARON FURMAN

"Jeff Faust broke our Scoutmaster's finger in a tubing accident and then took his place in the Scoutmaster Splash wearing a full Class A uniform."

SETH BRAUNSTEIN

"Pulling off ticks, lots of ticks; watching Marshyhope Creek mud get scraped off a flesh wound; seeing someone drive into a tree, then drive away."

ALEX HAWTHORNE

"My son was learning to ride a bike. He ran into a holly bush. To this day, he swears the bush jumped in front of him."

CHRIS GONZALEZ

"Hiking through waist-deep water on the red trail! I plunged in and the troop followed!"

CHRISTOPHER CULLEN

"I never drank coffee before becoming the camp commissioner. You walk around and talk to people and they constantly say, 'Would you like a cup of coffee?' I kept saying no, no. Then I realized I'm being rude to these people, so I started drinking coffee. Just haven't stopped yet."

LEE MURDOCH

"When we greeted leaders in the old admin building, they would be greeted by a fire in the fireplace and chairs circling the hearth. Everyone turned in their rosters and prepared for the leaders' meeting. Great company and true Scouters."

RAY BERTRAND

"When I was here for Cub resident camp, our staff guide said if one of us scored three bullseyes on the archery range, he would dress up in pink and dance across the stage on closing campfire saying 'I'm a pretty princess! I'm a pretty princess!' and he stayed true to that promise after I scored all three bullseyes."

PAUL DEREPENTIGNY

"Campfire slideshows with Ray Teat soundtracks. Obsessed with wilderness survival, knots, constantly covered in soot, evening program, friends for life, working hard and playing harder."

HENRY CLIFFORD

"It never rains at camp. It's liquid sunshine. For the summers I worked there, I spent a lot of time jumping in puddles. There were few things I loved more than soaking my uniforms in the huge, marshy puddles that formed around camp – particularly out in the activities field and right by the administration building/Brownsea. We formed a little Olympic Puddling Jumping team of folks who tended to splash more than others and spent our time recruiting for the team. One by one we got other staff to give in and go big into the mess. One particular day, amidst a crabby week, we got Lee Murdoch, Dave Chew, and Greg Morris to belly flop into the puddles. Their faces wore pure joy, until the sand settled into their shorts and they recalled why they hadn't surrendered to our pressure before that."

JILL PRICE

"Pulling up to the dusty parking lot and being attacked by hordes of deer flies and sheep flies!"

CHARLES SHAEFF

"One time I was hiking with Dave Harris, and we'd gone out past Red Banks. He and I were just walking, be-bopping along, and both of us froze in mid-stride. Both of us had this just really creepy feeling, and we kind of looked at each other. I said, 'I don't feel right,' and Dave said the same thing. We both turned around and ran the whole way back to camp."

GENE STERLING

"One time I was pulling a waterskiier, and he fell off the skis and of course I stopped the boat. But when I stopped, there was a water snake coming up right beside him. I saw the snake, but he didn't – it's a good thing, because it might have scared him to death!"

RAY APPLER

"Driving down the long winding road."

CHANDLER SICKMUND

There is no teaching
to compare with example.

ROBERT BADEN-POWELL

Part Five:
Summer Staff

Hiring staff is described by one camp director as the most important and challenging part of their job. Not everyone wants to give up an entire summer to work in a buggy, humid marshland for relatively little pay while living in a tent or rustic cabin. But each year, calls and applications come in and the staff assembles into a team.

The vast majority of program staff today are former campers. The staff actively recruits Scouts and Venturers while they attend camp, and encourages them to apply for positions in the future.

Paul DeRepentigny, the 2019 program director, said he was urged to apply for a staff job by a Handicrafts instructor. "I really looked up to him. We were working on a project in pottery together, and I was showing another kid what we were doing ... He said, 'You look like you could teach this. You could become a staff member,'" DeRepentigny recalled. "It had never occurred to me before that."

Mark Dyer Sr., who was trading post manager as a 16-year-old Scout in 1984, recalled sending in his application to Camp Director Bob Steele and writing "negotiable" for his requested salary. "He called me up and said, 'What's negotiable mean?' I said, 'Just what it says.'" The strategy apparently paid off for Dyer, who earned $450 that summer.

Some staff were hired on the spot as campers, like Chris Arbeene, tapped to be a counselor-in-training the summer of 1998. A rousing performance of "I'm A Little Teapot" at the closing campfire earned him a job offer for the rest of the summer and two more years on the aquatics staff. "I literally came home that Saturday, washed all my stuff, repacked all my stuff, and came to work the following day," he said.

For Lee Murdoch, it was his older brother, Billy, who spurred him to apply in the spring of 1995. "I was more content to play video games and sleep on the couch than I was to work," he recalled. "One day, my brother very frankly and emphatically said, 'What are you going to do with the rest of your life, sleep on this couch?' And that sort of woke up a part of me. I was one of those late additions to the roster. I had taken sailing lessons and knew how to fish, so I had the opportunity to teach sailing, help out with canoeing, and help out with swimming.

"I got really motivated there about working and creating my own identity. … I didn't know it at the time, but going to work on summer camp staff in 1995 was really the start of me forging my own path, personally and professionally in a lot of ways."

Several roles, like directors of the aquatics, shooting sports and climbing programs, require specialized qualifications and training, including age requirements – being at least 21 years old. That can make those positions tougher to fill.

Scott Cheesman, who had a key role in hiring as program director for three years, said he looked first for maturity and second for personality. "Skills, we can learn that," he said. "You want someone who's mature enough to realize that they're going to be considered an adult."

Murdoch, who headed the hiring process as both program director and camp director, said he also looked for inner qualities. "Part of it is, 'Do I think that they're going to be a part of the culture? Do I think that they're going to be willing to learn? Do I think that they're going to be willing to push themselves to be the best?' …

"When you're interviewing young camp staff members, you've got to look through the tendency of a 14- or 15-year-old sitting in an office with adults in an interview to be timid and soft-spoken. You've got to look through that, and you've got to be willing to take a chance on somebody."

Staff members are given a tremendous amount of responsibility for their young age. Henry Clifford remembered going to National Camp School for training as head commissioner, returning with the knowledge that at other camps, there were separate staffs for Scoutcraft and first-year camper programs – but at Henson in the 1990s, the commissioners did the jobs of three staffs. "It's funny to think that you're 18 years old and you're in charge of all this stuff," he said. "But Ray didn't ask anybody to run a program who wasn't capable of rising to the occasion."

"In hindsight, it's a really scary thing," joked Murdoch. "We're entrusted with a plethora of axes, hatchets, knives, fuel-starting mechanisms, and given a group of young men to shape their minds and go on these wilderness adventures?"

Jeff Faust, who would go on to work at camp for many summers, found his way to Nanticoke Road as a bored teenager on a bicycle. He and his mother spent summers in Sharptown with his future stepfather, and Faust would cycle around the town with nothing to do. "One day I was like, 'Holy crap! There's a whole camp here,' " he recalled. "It was really just curiosity with a little bit of happenstance and dumb luck."

Many repeat staff members have a "rock star" moment that keeps them coming back, DeRepentigny noted: "My first year on staff, I had no idea what I was doing and I was kind of nervous. I taught Soil and Water Conservation, a tiny, tiny merit badge. The only people who signed up were from a troop in Virginia, and they just completely adored me. Every year they've come back, they've been shouting my name whenever they see me and signing up for all my classes. It really adds to the experience if you're able to make those connections to the Scouts and start coming back for them."

In some cases, multiple generations of families have spent time at camp, including on staff. There's perhaps no better example than the Sterlings, with a father and three sons on the rosters – and a grandfather who was a unit leader the first year camp opened.

Kevin Sterling remembered picking up his older brother, Gene, from his CIT interview weekend one winter. "The whole parking lot seemed to be empty because everyone else had already left. And my brother was sweeping the front porch – and he kept sweeping, and sweeping, and sweeping and I thought to myself, 'Good God, what a brown-noser.' He wanted them to see how hard he was willing to work to be a part of the staff there," Kevin Sterling remembered. "In retrospect, I think that says a lot about his character."

"Going into the admin building and seeing all the names on the walls, it's almost like a family tree," reflected Gene Sterling. "Ideally, one day my kids will get to go there."

Counselors-In-Training

A good CIT program helps identify future instructors and area directors; nurtures young staff members in leadership development; introduces them to camp culture; and enhances the camper experience by providing enthusiastic, energetic role models for campers to emulate closer to their age.

The CIT program at Henson has proved a substantial success in those areas. Many longtime staff members began their careers as campers and moved into a CIT role when they were eligible at ages 14-15. CITs traditionally have rotated through multiple program areas and support services roles, helping with instruction and seeing how camp works behind the scenes. In some cases, CITs under 16 did a two-year stint in that role before being hired as full-time instructors or support staff.

"CITs have a rough gig," observed Chris Jensen. "They're dealing with kids sometimes older than they are. But the CITs have been trained more – we're just giving them more knowledge and then expecting them to be able to teach it."

CITs often look up to senior staff in what sometimes approaches hero worship. Many had a sharp focus on the program area they wanted to be placed in when they were able to join the full paid staff ranks. For many years during Cub Scout resident camp, CITs were assigned to serve as "program specialists," leading Cub dens around camp, assisting with program, leading songs and games, and being a den chief-like resource to the parents and adult leadership.

"It was the first time to figure out myself in a completely brand-new situation," Scott Cheesman recalled of his CIT year in 2001. "It was probably the thing in life that got me the most ready for life. You're in a new social group that's almost completely a new thing, and you're in this weird hierarchical structure where you're in charge of a lot but you're also in charge of nothing. You learn to be very responsible without having control."

More than 300 young men and women have served as counselors-in-training at Henson over the years. The first identified as a CIT, Tom Callahan, showed up on the staff rolls in 1967. There were no CITs recorded during much of the 1960s, a few years in the 1970s, or the early 1980s. But by the mid-80s, CITs were signing up left and right, and the number boomed especially after 2005. The record was 16 CITs in 2007, 2008 and 2013.

The CIT ranks are dotted with youngsters who would go on to many years on paid staff, including Brian Schmidt (1988), Billy Murdoch (1990 and 1991), Jeff Faust (1992), Aaron Furman (1994), Kevin Sterling (1998), Greg Morris (1999), Logan Rosenberg (1999), Scott Cheesman (2001), Emerson Sklar (2001), Charlie Mitchell (2002), Frankie Sears (2002), Ryan Teat (2004 and 2005), Paul Brady (2005), Matt Winebrenner (2006 and 2007), Andrew Solomon (2007), Jean-Paul Koushel (2009), and Jimmy Chaparro (2013).

Veteran staff member Bill Sterling, a CIT in 1966-67, summed it up well: "No pay, but an incredible experience."

Women On Staff

Despite the national organization's name, women have played an integral role in the history of the camp from the beginning. Records note that the first woman on staff was Margaret Lewis, who worked in the health lodge in 1968, three years after camp opened. Women also filled jobs as camp cook, kitchen aide, and camp clerk. In 1974, Hazel Cook, wife of staff member Homer Cook, joined the support services staff, where she worked in various capacities for four years. Another Hazel, Hazel Upton, worked on staff as a health officer or volunteer for six years in the 1980s and 1990s.

In 1985, Nancy Webb took up the post of camp cook, a position she would hold for a decade. A beloved member of the staff, she served as a camp mother to many young staff members. Her culinary creations helped fuel program staff during setup and teardown.

Angie Olds was hired as the first woman to serve on program staff, in 1975, teaching archery and field sports. Her husband, Keith, worked in aquatics. The first female area director appears to have been Amy Green, in 1982, leading aquatics. The first female program director was Lisa Lancaster in 1989. That was the same year changes also were occurring nationally, as women were allowed into direct unit-leader positions with the Boy Scout program and were also approved to join the Order of the Arrow.

"Scouting has become more and more inclusive over the years, and as adult leadership of units grow and change their expectations change," Teat said.

The first female counselors-in-training were Cierra Mohr and Harley Werner, staff members in 2016. And in 2019, the Boy Scout program changed nationally to Scouts BSA, opening all of the BSA's youth programs up to both girls and boys.

Staff Week

For decades, Staff Week has been an essential part of summer staff life at Henson. On paper, it's the week prior to the opening of camp, when staff report for six straight days of training, campsite setup, and program area prep. In reality, Staff Week is when vital bonds are forged and friendships made for life. Staff members spend time doing physical labor – hauling and setting up platforms, 4x4s, outriggers, poles and canvas – as well as time reviewing camp policies and procedures, getting skills training, writing lesson plans, and role-playing how to help campers.

At its core, Staff Week creates tight bonds, said 19-year veteran Chris Jensen. "Just the camaraderie of setting up camp puts the team together," he said. "At the beginning of the week, everyone's uncomfortable with each other; the middle of the week, when you start breaking out into program areas, everybody has regular friends. … You get some competition with one crew doing better than the others – it's fun, it's work."

Eric Salser said that competition sometimes went to extremes, such as how much staff would load the camp vehicles with tent supplies. "It was always a challenge to see just how many platforms we could stack. I'm surprised nobody got hurt with that dumb haywagon," he said. "Henry Clifford was about 6'7" so his reach was darn near 10 feet, and Billy Murdoch was a pretty tall guy, too. We used to see just how high we could get them, and there were a couple times when you couldn't move that haywagon hardly at all – the bottom of the wagon was dragging on the tires as we pulled it around."

"I remember just the hard work that it involved – getting out there and just sweating, putting the tents up over and over and over and over again, and enjoying the spirit of working with great people," Henry Clifford said. "You got a lot of respect for that – an appreciation for just doing a job well done and working hard."

One staff member who had been a camper for several summers recalled getting a shiver down his spine while sorting through the old olive-drab wooden chests that held program supplies and equipment for the first time. "This was the real deal – we were actually running program," he remembered. "Being a camper never prepared me for that feeling."

For many years, the half-week transition between Scouts BSA and Cub Scout camp was the chance to re-train and re-focus program areas for the needs of Cubs. The axes, ATVs, shotguns and sailboats went into storage, and staff got a special orientation on the rhythms of Cub camp, including constant songs and games.

Some years, staff week has been partly elongated, with area directors arriving a few days in advance and the top administrators arriving a few days before them. That was part of Murdoch's strategy to prepare the camp for the staff. "We set up Tent City, we cleaned up the Longhouse, we made sure all the things were the way we expected camp to look," he said. "When staff arrived, we positioned area directors at staff housing sites to welcome them and help them unload their cars – little touches that were very intentional with the idea that the staff is our most valuable customer. If we take care of the staff, they'll take care of the campers."

One challenge, DeRepentigny noted, has been that some younger staff members are still in high school when staff week begins. That forces the leadership to sometimes push the start of the camping season back a week.

DeRepentigny said the bonding experiences are vitally important, but skills training and general staff orientation are also necessary, especially for staff members who have never been Scouts. "Not everyone knows the patrol system, let alone how to teach it to other people," he said.

The pre-camp period begins a lot earlier, of course, for the administration team, which has been planning for the summer sessions for months if not longer. Program area directors who need certification – such as aquatics, climbing, shooting sports, outdoor skills and nature/ecology – also start earlier with a week at National Camp School, where they get essential training in their jobs and how to meet national camp standards.

"Camp isn't all bubbles and laughs – it's hard, gritty, unpredictable to some degree," said Jill Price. "But time and experience proves a great camp staff can navigate all those things together and end up smiling. I loved the training weeks to help prepare us for all of it – the good, the bad, and the ugly weeks of midsummer doldrum."

The Red Roost

For many years, the summer staff has kept up the tradition of a visit to a Whitehaven crabhouse known as the Red Roost, built from a converted chicken house. There are all-you-can-eat crabs, fried chicken, corn and hush puppies; it's a rustic establishment, with squeeze bottles of butter and rolls of paper towels on the tables.

It's a special highlight for many staffers – a chance to eat good food, to be sure, but also an opportunity for camaraderie and fun while not wearing the uniform. The centerpiece of the evening has been song night, which is just what it sounds like: A band plays at the front of the dining area, while staff members lead the restaurant in a rousing chorus of camp songs. It's an experience that defies description.

"One night, we sang 'You've Lost That Loving Feeling' to our waitress," Chris Arbeene remembered. "I don't know who was more embarrassed by that, the waitress or us."

"A lot of my fond memories are from that mid-summer visit to the Red Roost, just being there, seeing everybody in their 'normal clothes,' and just having fun singing songs, being a little silly," said Lee Murdoch. "One year, I talked to an older couple there, and they said, 'Oh, yeah, we put this on the calendar every year. We love to come when the Boy Scouts are here. You guys have such a great time.' I would think that some diners would be pretty agitated by a group of 70 folks rolling in, singing camp songs at the top of their lungs, but they just loved it."

Staff Life

The saying "work hard, play hard" is embodied in camp staff. Whether staying in Tent City, the Longhouse, the Family Cabins or another building around camp, staff came loaded for the summer with trunks, fans, carpets, video game consoles, and all the comforts of home.

"We had all sorts of stuff in our tents – everything from blacklights to posters. You would have thought we were in actual cabins with all the power strips we had running through them," said Chris Arbeene, a staff member in the late 1990s. He and staffer Matt Gonce even brought their instruments to camp and created a mini-band: "He was playing guitar, I was playing my drums, and we were jamming out to Nirvana on our nights off, just a bunch of '90s grunge kids."

Staff life some years involved nights off at the Sharptown Firemen's Carnival, or in Ocean City at a go-kart track or under-21 nightclub – "being a teenager and just screwing around," as one staffer put it.

"It was kind of nutty, because by the time you got off, you got signed out, you got in somebody's car, you had finagled your mom to say it was OK to go, and then you left … it was a two-hour process to have 60 minutes in Ocean City," chuckled Gene Sterling.

One evening in the late 1990s, a handful of staffers went to the mall in Salisbury and got their ears pierced with platinum studs (of course earning the collective nickname "The Platinum Studs"). They sat in a line the next morning at breakfast facing the door to Teat's office. He walked into the dining area, saw the row of smiling faces with gleaming earrings, shook his head, and walked back out.

Shenanigans of various sorts were also prevalent. Multiple staff members told stories of sneaking out of camp late at night for an illicit evening out – honing their night vision so they could drive quietly past the ranger's house with headlights off. Alpert remembered one trip to Ocean City in 1985 when he and other staff members pushed a Ford Pinto down the road to sneak past new Ranger Ray Teat. "Once we got it far enough, we started it and on we went," Alpert recalled. "We were supposed to come back the same night, but we fell asleep. We got back the next morning and everyone was having breakfast. That wasn't good."

Jill Price recalled taking naps while tethered onto the top of the climbing tower her first summer working COPE. "I needed naps that first summer because I stayed up playing Spades at night in Alder Lodge with some of the older guys on staff. Night after night we plopped down at a table after night program ended. Tent City boys went to their sleeping quarters, Dana went to bed, and I went to play cards until we ate all the snacks and drained the last laughs.

"My very first Saturday off I slept 15 hours on my top bunk, drool all caked on my face. I had never worked or played so hard in a week's time until then."

Many staff members, even those from decades past, speak about those summer days in tones of reverence. "Every small part played by each staff member was so important," recalled former aquatics director Rob Kulewicz, who worked on staff in the mid-1990s. "I will forever be indebted to everyone I met and was lucky enough to spend time with during those summers."

For many people who served on staff and have since been scattered across the country, raising families of their own, returning to camp would be a rare but much-welcomed opportunity, even for just a single day. Murdoch, who at the time of this writing was the newly-minted Scout Executive for the Conquistador Council in New Mexico, summed the prospect up well:

> I'd of course want to enjoy a cup of coffee in the morning on the porch in a rocking chair, visit that cedar tree at the chapel and offer a prayer for all the future campers and staff that'll visit the camp, take a hike out into the woods, build a lean-to fire, watch a flag ceremony, enjoy dinner with friends, and then silently enjoy the sunset and remember all the laughs and friends and campfires past at the waterfront.

> I look forward to this day so much, as at this point I'm a distant memory to most, if not all camp staff members. So I'd have the chance to blend in and be another dad taking his daughter to camp and seeing the beauty and the excitement through her eyes.

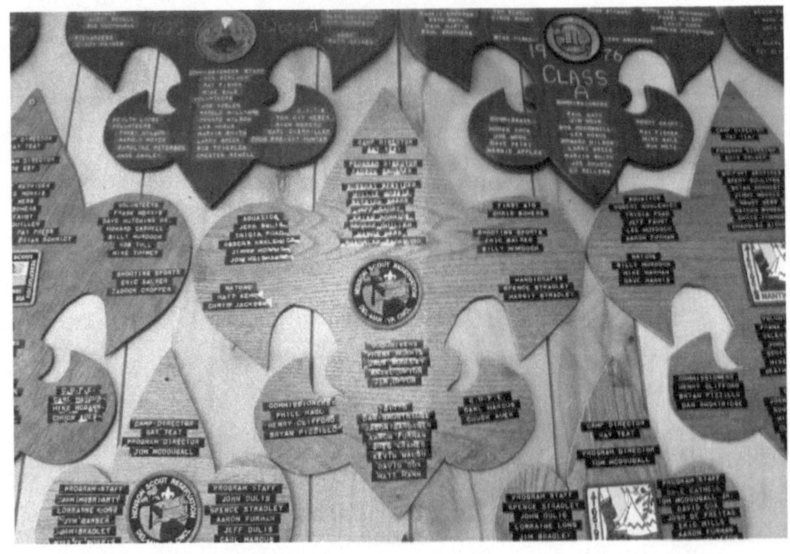

Summer Staff Lists

Nanticoke's staff is an intensely devoted group. For many, working on summer staff isn't just any other job — it's a way of life. Hundreds of people have worked on staff over the years. Nearly 100 people have worked on summer staff for five years or more. Of those, sixteen have worked for 10 years or more.

The following lists were transcribed from the staff plaques that hang in the Administration Building lounge. Minor corrections have been made to known spelling errors, but otherwise the list represents the official record of the summer camp staff. Any errors in transcription or organization are that of the author. Staff are listed by year, then alphabetically by last name.

1965

John Baildon
Jim Britton
John Britton
Tom Britton
Jim Clark
Dave Disborough
Buck Duncan
Jim Foster
Ken Gerlach

Shep Henry
Herb Hurst
Jim Hutto
Jim Johnson
Larry Jones
Pat Massa
Jeff McBriety
Steve Nagley
Ira Nelson

Edward Newman
Ken Olsen
Jean Perusse
Jim Pooley
Win Taylor
Drew Uhde
Kruger

1966

Kirk Beits
Al Betts
Bill Boyette
Donn Brinkley
Jim Britton
John Britton
Jim Byrd
George Cameron
Gene Caven
Phil Chabot
Jim Clark

Buck Duncan
Ken Gerlach
Tom Hars
Shep Henry
Greg Hill
John Horner
Steve Horoszko
Herb Hurst
Larry Jones
Pat Massa
Glen Mumford

Jean Perusse
Jim Pooley
Craig Reynolds
Jim Richardson
Chester Sewell
Jay Sloane
Bill Sterling
Frank Wallace
John Williams
Tom Willing

1967

Bill Bloodsworth
Bill Bodenstab
Charles Bosch
Donn Brinkley
Jim Britton
John Britton
Tom Callahan
Jim Clark
Tim Conley
Buck Duncan
Larry Farlow

John Halterman
Tom Hennima
Shep Henry
Don Higgins
Indian Joe
Don Jones
Keith Kahl
Clen Mumford
George Murphey
Everett Oppenheimer

Gary Outten
Noland Pase
Craig Reynolds
Jay Sloane
Bill Sterling
Keith Ulrich
Frank Wallace
Bob West
Gordon Wheatley
Jim Wilson

1968

Michael Baker
Don Brinkley
Tom Callahan
Tom Haas
Tom Henning
Shep Henry

John Horner
Cliff Lewis
Margret Lewis
Bennie Ma
Ken Olsen
Bert Perdue

Craig Reynolds
Charles Shaeff
Bill Sterling
Jim Urse
Frank Wallace
Dick Winchell

1969

Joe Belet
Tom Callahan
Robert Cameron
David Daudt
Donald Enslen
Roger Gulick
Robert Henry
Shep Henry
David Kahlbaugh
Clifton Lewis
Margaret Lewis

Richard
Meinersmann
John Mitchell
Paul Neer
Joe O'Day
David Olsen
Kenneth Olsen
Dwayne Powell
James F.
Richardson
Jim Richardson

Karl Schlatter
Joe Schwartz
Charles Sewell
Charles Shaeff
Bill Sterling
Harrell Stokes
James Urse
Bob Wood
Dennis Yancy

1970

Lars Arnesson
J. Spicer Bell
Tom Callahan
Bob Cameron
Bruce Cameron
Don Cameron
Chris Effinger
Scott Ewing
Greg Fogle
Dave Godfrey
Chris Henry

Shep Henry
Jim Lappen
Clifton Lewis
Marge Lewis
Rick Meinsermann
Tim Meredith
Jon Mitchell
Wayne Norton
Jim O'Day
Joe O'Day
Jeff Pagano

Nolan Pase
Jim Richardson
Jim F. Richardson
Jim Rowe
Charles Sewell
Charles Shaeff
Hugh Smith
Bill Sterling
Harrell Stokes

1971

Bruce Cameron
Don Cameron
George Clendaniel
Bill Cover
Bob Fraze
Kristian Graversgaard-Knudsen
Howard Guth
Chris Henry
Shep Henry
Pat Hodges
Herb Hurst
Mrs. Knepshield
Les McClung
Glen Mumford
Francis Nichols Jr.
Wayne Norton
Jeff Pagano
Bruce Phillips
John Pizzadili
James Prisco
David Ramia
Jim Rowe
Bill Sterling
Dave Swab
Paul Touart
Steve Touart
Dick Winchell
Jimmy Winchell
Ann Zimmer
Don Zimmer

1972

Allen Barnes
Bruce Cameron
Don Cameron
Bill Cann
Bob Cohen
Homer Cook
Shirley Cook
Karen Dahl
Andrew Ednie
Dave Fullerton
Jeff Harris
Shep Henry
Mark Kearney
Frank Kelly
Mrs. Knepshield
Bob Lomax
Carl Malmberg
Carl Martin
Jim McBriety
Keith Olds
Scott Peters
John Pizzadili
Jim Richardson
Kenny Roach
Jim Rowe
Takashi Taguchi
Ann Zimmer
Don Zimmer

1973

Bob Adams	Clent Lowe	Tom Smith
Linda Adams	Tom McCabe	Lance Stracke
J.C. Collins	Suisei Musgrave	Ed Waterland
Mike Connelly	Keith Olds	Bob Webster
Homer Cook	Chuck Olsen	Gary White
Andrew Ednie	Scott Peters	Ann Zimmer
Shep Henry	Jim Richardson	Don Zimmer
Paul Lemke	Jim F. Richardson	Molly (Camp Dog)
Kun-Hae Liu	Kenny Roach	Pepper (Camp Dog)

1974

Darrell Baker	Ana Jimenez	Jim Rowe
Linda Barrows	Joerg Leinemann	Thomas E. Smith
Tom Barrows	Shaun Looby	Tom R. Smith
Barry Chevalier	Clent Lowe	Roger Street
Hazel Cook	Tim Meredith	Bill Torrey
Homer L. Cook	Mark Newton	Ed Westerland
Tackie Cropper	Bill Nuttle	Gary White
Dan Eliason	Scott Peters	Ann Zimmer
George B. Fitzgerald	Kenny Roach	Don Zimmer
	Eric Roth	

1975

Bill Barnhill	Les Hogue	Caroline Peterson
Bill Brown	Doug Hunter	Eric Roth
Jane Cawley	Don Kelly	Chester Sewell
Dave Clark	Joe Koeler	Kerry Sewell
Tackie Cropper	Glen Mayfield	Charlie Shaeff
Bob Custard	Bob McConnell	Marvin Smith
Ray Fisher	Guy Metz	Seiji Sugiura
Mike Gale	Harold Moyer	Jim Thompson
Ken Gerlach	John Murrell	Bob Triesler
Larry Greer	Rich Nadeau	Mike Vincent
Cindy Haines	Angie Olds	Tom Weber
Ruth Haines	Keith Olds	Harold Williams
Ed Harriman	Carl Overmiller	Howard Wilson
Shep Henry	Chip Parman	Pansy Wilson

1976

Lena Anderson	Les Hogue	Ed Sellers
Herb Appler	Paul Martin	Tom Sewell
Paul Brothers	Bob McConnell	Charlie Shaeff
Dennis Brown	Norma Lee	Vince Short
Dave Clark	McConnell	Marvin Smith
Homer Cook	Guy Metz	Doug Stewart
Lanie Corn	Jim Moir	Joe Swartz
Tackie Cropper	Chip Parmen	Bob Triesler
Ray Fisher	Dave Petry	Mike Vincent
Mike Gale	Carolyn Petterson	Paul Wade
Larry Greer	Bob Reynolds	Howard Wilson
Ed Harriman	Mike Riall	Pansy Wilson
Shep Henry	Eric Roth	Joe Wood

1977

Jim Barber
Ray Blades
Steve Blessing
John Burgess
Jim Campbell
Hazel Cook
Homer Cook
Mat Dullaghan
Bob Eliason
Jim Fleming
Mike Gale
Barbara Green
Randy Green

Shep Henry
Les Hogue
Lesli Jack
Ken Keiser
Eric Knospe
Paul McLaughlin
Greg Moir
Jim Moir
C.C. Moore
Dan Oliphant
Chris Pease
Bruce Peterson
Carolyn Peterson

John Pollock
Steve Putscher
Jon Rohrer
Mark Roth
Ed Sellers
Marvin Smith
Spence Stradley
Andy Strouse
John Suratt
Jerry Taylor
Kevin Thomas
Paul Wade
Ann Zimmer

1978

Herb Appler
Ray Appler
Tom Campbell
Virginia Capel
Gail Cawley
David Clark
Hazel Cook
Homer Cook
Barry Dengler
David Detwiler
Jeff Eldridge
George Fitzgerald
Ken Gerlach
John Green

Dwayne Griffin
Shep Henry
Rosemary Hickman
Les Hogue
Kevin Les Callette
Bob Lomax
Roger Maki
Greg Moir
Jim Moir
In-Taek Moon
Carolyn Peterson
Jim Richardson
Mary Richardson
Jason Ross

Mark Roth
Ed Sellers
Tom Sewell
Ken Short
Glenn Silbert
Marvin Smith
Mark Stenger
Keith Stephens
Spence Stradley
Kevin Thomas
Keith Tolson
Reed Townsend
Paul Wade
Jim Wills

1979

Larry Bartz	Chris Huener	Carol Peterson
Tom Campbell	Eric Knospe	Mary Pulnock
Bill Cantara	Jeff Lane	Mark Roth
Virginia Capel	Kevin Les Callette	Bob Salser
Archie Cawley	Bob Lomax	Ed Sellers
Hazel Cook	Bob McConnell	Tom Sewell
Homer Cook	Pat McCoy	Joanne Stephens
Philip Crouse	Bill McDonald	Spence Stradley
Clark Droney	Jim Moir	Keith Tolson
Buddy Dunn	Frank Mott	Carl Voss
Amy Green	Keith Patterson	Joan Voss
Eric Green	Gil Perdue	Emma Jean Wilson
Joe Green	Bruce Peterson	

1980

Rich Altemus	Tracy Gibb	Kurt Roth
Herb Appler	Joe Green	Bob Salser
Jane Burt	Tim Hanrahan	Bill Schlegal
John Burt	Tim Hanrahan	Ed Sellers
Tom Campbell	Earl Jones	Tom Sewell
Bill Cantara	Kevin Les Callette	Tom Sewell
Doris Cantara	Eric Martin	Randall Smith
Wayne Cawley	Bob McConnell	Joann Stephens
Bill Coffin	Tom McDermit	Larry Thomas
Phil Crouse	Bill Mitchell	Keith Tolson
Buddy Dunn	John Myers	Betsy VanCulin
Bob Finney	Joe Nudge	Joan Voss
George Fitzgerald	Gil Perdue	Emma Jean Wilson
Bob Gell	Chuck Ruebeck	Harold Wilson

1981

Dean Altemus
Rich Altemus
Tom Campbell
Bill Cantara
Bill Coffin
Tracy Gibb
Joe Gibbons
Amy Green
Don Hall
Dave Hartman

Dan Howell
Gardner Jackson
Ed Lawson
Kevin Les Callette
Mike Lokey
Eric Martin
Jim Mueller
John Myers
Keith Paterson
Gil Perdue

Steve Reed
Paul Roehrig
Kurt Roth
Chuck Ruebeck
Steve Schwartz
Ed Sellers
Joanne Stephens
Emma Jean Wilson

1982

John Brady
Bill Cantara
Bob Finney
Tracey Gibb
Amy Green
Steve Grutzik
Steve Grutzik
John Hinspeter
John Hopwood
Scott Jones

Kevin Les Callette
Mike Lokey
Eric Martin
Chris McNeal
Phil Mesibov
Kevin Morris
Keith Patterson
Gil Perdue
Paul Peters
Mary Pufnock

Fred Sayin
Carl Schuchardt
Steve Shepherd
Rich Stahlhut
Joanne Stephens
Pat Stoops
Kathy Tingle
Mark Trego

1983

Chris Baum
Bill Cantara
Bob Dechene
John Deming
Brian Deshon
Jeff Dulis
Jerold Dulis
Tom Farrell
Royal Johnson
Ralph Kimes

Mike Lokey
Bill Maass
Rhonda McLaughlin
John McNally
Ed Morgan
Bud Nichols
John Oelfke
Paul Peters
Joe Rezac

Fred Sayin
Steve Schwartz
Sanjay Sharma
Bob Steele
Joanne Stephens
Kathy Tingle
Mark Trego
Larry Wagner
Tom Zizileuskas

1984

Ray Bertrand
Dave Brown
John Davis
Bob Dechene
Jeff Dulis
Jerold Dulis
Mark Dyer
Amy Hartmann
Dave Hartmann
Dave Hartmann
Ralph Kimes

Ben Lonski
Regina Maffia
Elly Mateo
John Oelfke
Bert Perdue
Rita Pryor
Joe Rezac
Ed Sellers
B-J Simmons
Brian Snyder
Bob Steele

Jamie Steele
Josh Steele
Wendy Steele
Margit Stradley
Spence Stradley
Ray Teat
Louie Timmons
Hazel Upton
Danny Wallace
Myron Worley
Vincent Worley

1985

Guy Banks	Ralph Kimes	Bruce Summers
Ray Bertrand	Elly Mateo	Ray Teat
Bob Dechene	Kevin Nagiyski	Hazel Upton
Jerold Dulis	Mia Nelson	Nancy Webb
George Fleckenstein	John Oelfke	Steve Wilcoxon
	Jim Robinson	Myron Worley
Amy Hartmann	Lee Rosinoski	Vinnie Worley
Detlef Hartmann	Ed Sellers	

1986

Billy Brown	Leif Hancock	Joe Stockly
Jim Byrd	Cliff Jones	Bruce Summers
John Conner	Tom Kennish	Ray Teat
Bob Dechene	Butch King	Joe Toro
Jeff Dulis	Larry King	Hazel Upton
Jerold Dulis	Ben Lonski	Scott Venables
George Fleckenstein	Don Lonski	Nancy Webb
	Kevin Nagyski	Denise Wolverton
Mary Fleckenstein	Rich Parsons	Vinnie Worley
Paul Freebery	Tim Patterson	
Bobby Hamilton	Kevin Ritchie	

1987

Ray Appler	Ty Hiter	Mark Rothchild
Brian Burd	Scott Jones	Ian Shortman
Bill Coffin	Cathy Kennish	Margit Stradley
Valerie Crank	Tom Kennish	Spence Stradley
Bob Dechene	Butch King	Ray Teat
Jill Green	Bruce Larmore	Hazel Upton
Joe Green	Blase Maffia	Jay Viers
John Gutierrez	Frank Morris	Nancy Webb
Bobby Hamilton	Tim Patterson	Yancy Wharton
Amy Hartmann	Frank Peters	Bill Whisler
Dave Hartmann	Jim Reis	Bob Williamson

1988

Herb Appler	Leah Johnson	Elizabeth Rose
Ray Appler	Phil Jones	Mark Rothschild
Jim Bird	Cathi Kazimir	Lee Rusanowsky
Ric Boston	Eric Kazimir	Desmond Sam
Mark Bumgarner	Butch King	Ricky Sasse
Nina Bumgarner	Bruce Larmore	Brian Schmidt
Brian Burd	Blase Maffia	Don Sheline
John Coddington	Richard Parsons	Carolyn Stange
Valerie Crank	Tim Patterson	Brent Sullivan
Carl Dreisbach	Frank Peters	Ray Teat
Charles Hiter	Hunter Phillips	Nancy Webb
Ty Hiter	Rob Robinson	Mike Zizilueskas

1989

Herb Appler	Phil Jones	Frank Peters
Allen Barnes	Cathie Kazimir	Hunter Phillips
Brian Burd	Eric Kazimir	Lee Rusanowsry
John Coddington	Butch King	Brian Schmidt
Valerie Crank	Lisa Lancaster	Brian Sharp
Jeff Dulis	Pat Lenz	Don Sheline
John Gutierrez	Catherine Lynch	Brent Sullivan
Danny Hamilton	Jack Lynch	Ray Teat
Charles Hiter	Bill Murdoch IV	Hazel Upton
Ty Hiter	Keith Oney	Jim Upton
Susan Hookam	Kevin Oney	Nancy Webb
Leah Johnson	Tim Patterson	Yancy Wharton

1990

Herb Appler	Carl Marcus	Brian Sharp
Chris Bowers	Chris Marousek	Don Sheline
Eric Chapman	Andy Marsh	Paul Slack
David Clark	Frank Morris	Brent Sullivan
Shawn Cosgrove	Billy Murdoch	Tony Szabo
Carl Eaton	Will Mynarends	Ray Teat
James Farrington	Keith Oney	Dennis Thornton
George Fleckenstein	Kevin Oney	Hazel Upton
Brad Frey	Mavis Palmer	Jim Upton
Rod Harrison	Tim Patterson	Nancy Webb
Phil Jones	Hunter Phillips	Bill Whisler
Pat Lenz	Dan Rossetti	Bryan White
Jack Lynch	Luis Saez	
	Brian Schmidt	

1991

Chris Bowers	Carl Marcus	Luis Saez
Alan Brien	Andy Marsh	Eric Salser
Greg Bush	Peter McAdoo	Brian Schmidt
Shawn Cosgrove	Tony McHugh	Carolyn Stange
Brad Frey	Billy Murdoch	Luther Steinbiss
David Frieman	Keith Oney	Margit Stradley
Ian Grey	Don Ott	Spence Stradley
Zak Hart	Ron Patterson	Ray Teat
Mark Johnston	Suzi Piccini	Regina Teat
Phil Jones	George Quillen	Paul Walker
Matt Kemp	David Runk	Steve Walker
Jack Lynch	Virginia Saborit	Nancy Webb

1992

Jerry Allen	Peter Kubica	Eric Salser
Chris Bowers	Ga'Bor Lengyel	Jim Sampson
Greg Bush	Trent Lillis	Hansel Shieh
Henry Clifford	Jack Lynch	Chandler Sickmund
Zadock Cropper	Carl Marcus	Jeff Smith
Jeff Faust	Jason Miller	Margit Stradley
Dolf Groen	Frank Morris	Spence Stradley
Scott Hacking	Millie Morris	Ray Teat
Garry Harris	Billy Murdoch	Cherie Titerence
Zak Hart	Don Ott	Paul Watters
Tony Hughes	Rob Parsons	Nancy Webb
Dave Hutchins	Tricia Poad	Jon Whitney
Dave Jennings	Pat Press	
Matt Kemp	George Quillen	

1993

Chuck Auer	Dave Hutchins	Eric Salser
Chris Bowers	Dave Hutchins Sr.	Jim Sampson
Howard Caswell	Leah Johnson	Brian Schmidt
Aaron Clark	Mike Keene	Chandler Sickmund
Henry Clifford	Bob Kuklewicz	Jeff Smith
Zadock Cropper	Carl Marcus	Margit Stradley
Jim Davis	Mike McGann	Spence Stradley
David Dorr	Frank Morris	Ray Teat
Joe Eby	Millie Morris	Rob Tull
Jeff Faust	Billy Murdoch	Mike Turner
Howard Fooksman	Bryan Pizzillo	Nancy Webb
Jason Gardiner	Tricia Poad	Jon Weishaupt
J.P. Green	Pat Press	Jon Whitney
Phil Hall	George Quillen	Geof Zehnacker

1994

Chuck Auer	Rob Kuklewicz	Dan Shortridge
Chris Bowers	Matt Mann	Chandler Sickmund
Henry Clifford	Carl Marcus	Margit Stradley
David Cox	Frank Morris	Spence Stradley
Zadock Cropper	Jimmy Morris	Ray Teat
Jeff Dulis	Millie Morris	Hazel Upton
Jeff Faust	Billy Murdoch	Jim Upton
Aaron Furman	Bryan Pizzillo	Kevin Walsh
Jason Gardiner	Tricia Poad	Nancy Webb
Phil Hall	Pat Press	Jon Weishaupt
Chris Jackson	George Quillen	Jack Woolley
Matt Kemp	Eric Salser	
Greg Kramer	Brian Schmidt	

1995

Nathan Bonsall
Troy Bonsall
Chris Bowers
Soup Campbell
Henry Clifford
Mike Clifton
David Cox
Valerie Cox
Bob Dechene
Josh Defrietas
John Dulis
Jeff Faust
Aaron Furman
Paul Gleaton

Mike Harman
Dave Harris
Phil Jones
Heather Joslin
Rob Kuklewicz
Mike Lynch
Carl Marcus
Eric Mills
Frank Morris
Jimmy Morris
Billy Murdoch
G. Lee Murdoch
Brian Pizzillo
Tricia Poad

Clay Roberts
Eric Salser
Brian Schmidt
Dan Shortridge
Chandler Sickmund
Margit Stradley
Spence Stradley
Scott Stutz
Brent Sullivan
Ray Teat
Chris Timmons
Nancy Webb

1996

Ray Appler
Bob Batts
Nathan Bonsall
Tom Bonsall
Troy Bonsall
Soup Campbell
Henry Clifford
Mike Clifton
Steve Clifton
Dave Cox
Valerie Cox
Bob Dechene
Tim Dolch
Jed Doran
Eric Douglas
John Dulis

Chris Eccleston
Jeff Faust
Bobby Fehrman
Ed Freshwater
Aaron Furman
Paul Gleaton III
Dave Harris
Alex Hawthorne
Heather Joslin
Greg Kramer
Lorraine Long
Aaron Longfellow
Mike Love
Carl Marcus
Tom McDougall
Shyloh McIntyre

Bob Meader
Eric Mills
Billy Murdoch
G. Lee Murdoch
Kevin Nelson
Jason Raker
Clay Roberts
Eric Salser
Dan Shortridge
Gene Sterling
Margit Stradley
Spence Stradley
Brent Sullivan
Ray Teat
Brian Westfall

1997

Leon Barnhart
Nathan Bonsall
Tom Bonsall
Troy Bonsall
Michelle Brenneman
Mike Clifton
David Cox
Bob Dechene
Justin DeLaurier
Jed Doran
John Dulis
Chris Eccleston

Jeff Faust
Bobby Fehrman
Aaron Furman
Paul Gleaton Jr.
Dave Harris
Alex Hawthorne
Rob Kuklewicz
Mike Love
Rob Malone
Carl Marcus
Mike Masche
Tom McDougall
Andy Morris

G. Lee Murdoch
Don Ott
Austin Pick
Clay Roberts
Eric Salser
Dan Shortridge
Gene Sterling
Margit Stradley
Spence Stradley
Ray Teat
Tony Walker
Scott Watras

1998

Ray Appler
Chris Arbeene
Leon Barnhart
Jarred Bernstein
Laszlo Besze
Nathan Bonsall
Tom Bonsall
Troy Bonsall
Matt Chance
David Chew
Adam Copehaver
Dave Cox
Bob Dechene
John Dulis
Brian Eccleston
Chris Eccleston
Karen Eppheimer

Jeff Faust
Bobby Fehrman
Dave Harris
Alex Hawthorne
Grant Holt
Eric Hopkins
Gary Long
Charles LosCocco
Blase Maffia
Rob Malone
David Mars
Mike Masche
Tom McDougall
Bob Meader
Eric Mills
Andy Morris
G. Lee Murdoch

Bill Murdoch IV
Austin Pick
Jason Raker
John Renfro
Clay Roberts
Kennet Sampson
Don Sheline
Dan Shortridge
Kevin Sterling
Dana Teague
Ray Teat
Bob Watras
Scott Watras
Chris Webb
Matt Weisner
Kacper Wojzic

1999

Ray Appler
Chris Arbeene
Josh Bounds
Seth Braunstein
Michelle
Brenneman
Matt Chance
Dave Chew
Bob Dechene
Brian Eccleston
Chris Eccleston
Karen Eppeheimer
Jeff Faust
Bobby Fehrman
Troy Glessner
Matt Gonce
Billy Haines
Dave Harris
Alex Hawthorne
Erik Hopkins
Finith Jernigan
Ryan Karschner
Matt Krough
Blase Maffia
Tom McDougall
Zac Meilhammer
Andrew Miller
Greg Morris
G. Lee Murdoch
Mike Risser
Clay Roberts
Logan Rosenberg
Anastasia Segrit
Don Sheline
Oleg Shutov
Kevin Sterling
Dana Teague
Ray Teat
Aaron Vikor
Andrew Vogel
Byron White

2000

Yuri Anton
Ray Appler
Chris Arbeene
Jarred Bernstein
Josh Bounds
Seth Braunstein
Matt Chance
Dave Chew
Dimitri Dimitch
Brian Eccleston
Jeff Faust
Aaron Furman
Harvey Goins
Matt Gonce
Billy Haines
Dave Harris
Alex Hawthorne
John Hukill
Finith Jernigan
Aaron Kibler
Brian King
Anu Kornukova
Rob Malone
Tom McDougall
Zac Mielhammer
Andy Morris
G. Lee Murdoch
John Murray
Chris Nester
Cliff Nichols
Chris North
Dave Parks
Jill Price
Steve Rapczak
Clay Reister
Clay Roberts
Will Rooney
Logan Rosenberg
Jacob Schmidt
Andrew Stacey
Wayne Stacey
John Stephanos
Kevin Sterling
Spence Stradley
Dana Teague
Ray Teat
Natalia Tessa
Chris Thompson
Pritt Toomiste
Aaron Vikor
Andrew Vogel
Byron White
Kevin Willis

2001

Ray Appler	Matt Gonce	Cliff Nichols
Gergey Bartfai	Dave Harris	David Parks
Owen Bellis	T.J. Hodges	Jill Price
Jason Benton	Tara Hoffman	Nicky Quitter
Jarred Bondurant	John Hukill	Steve Rapczak
Josh Bounds	Jan Iraku	Will Rooney
Seth Braunstein	Chris Jensen	Logan Rosenberg
Matt Brenneman	Finith Jernigan	Emerson Sklar
Antonio Cercena	Matt Kemp	John Stephanos
Pavel Cernohorsky	Rusty Khaziyev	Ben Taylor
Scott Cheesman	Aaron Kibler	Dana Teague
David Chew	Nancy Lord	Ray Teat
Mike Deal	Rob Malone	Richard Thek
John Dulis	Tom McDougall	Justin Tuttle
Brian Eccleston	Jeff Moredock	Serge Valdzko
Jeff Faust	Greg Morris	Roman
Steve Faust	Tom Mroz	Vedoschenko
Gregory Gajdzicki	G. Lee Murdoch	Kevin Willis
Denis Golodnov	Don Murray	Husein Yanilmaz

2002

Owen Bellis
Jason Belote
Francis Boecker
Josh Bounds
Seth Braunstein
Charles Carson
Antonio Cercena
Scott Cheesman
Dave Chew
Aaron Chusid
Mike Deal
Jeff Faust
Marty Furbush
Mike Goins
Matt Gonce
T.J. Hodges
John Hukill
Chris Jensen
Devin Jernigan
Brian Klebon

Lucasz
Lewandowski
Nancy Lord
Joey McLaughlin
Charlie Mitchell
Greg Morris
Len Mueller
G. Lee Murdoch
Don Murray
Cliff Nichols
Tom Parent
David Parks
Michal Partyka
Paul Pisula
Cory Polidore
Charlie Pollard
Jill Price
Nicky Quitter
Steve Rapczak
Paul Razboikin

Will Rooney
Logan Rosenberg
Alex Salkov
Rob Sample
Frankie Sears
Andrey Serov
Ed Seward
Sam Sharp
Emerson Sklar
Marlie Smith
John Stephanos
Kevin Sterling
Dana Teague
Kara Teat
Ray Teat
Roman
Vedoschenko
Nic Vogel
Brian White
Michael Willis

2003

Artem Astrakhantsev
Cordairo Barnes
Jason Belote
Jason Benton
Seth Braunstein
Corby Burton
Frank Canter
Pavel Cernohorsky
Melik Ceyhun
Scott Cheesman
Dave Chew
Mike Deal
John Dulis
Karen Eppehimer
Olexiy Esavlov
Aaron Furman

Denis Golodnov
Matt Gonce
Shannon Gray
Dave Harris
T.J. Hodges
Chris Jensen
Finith Jernigan
Egor Kolpockov
Yury Kulikov
Rob Malone
Charlie Mitchell
Todd Morgan
Greg Morris
Millie Morris
G. Lee Murdoch
Cliff Nichols
Dave Parks

Jill Price
Steve Rapczak
Logan Rosenberg
Eric Salser
Rob Sample
Emerson Sklar
Bryan Stafford
Kevin Sterling
Brent Sullivan
Bob Swanson
Tim Swanson
Dana Teague
Kara Teat
Ray Teat
Franklin Wallace
John Woodington

2004

Adam Abruzzo
Elizabeth Appler
Ray Appler
Kevin Bailey
Cordairo Barnes
Wadde Barnes
Jarred Bernstein
John Bigony
Francis Boecker
Josh Boecker
Josh Bounds
Robert Bramble
Seth Braunstein
Pavel Cernohorsky
Scott Cheesman
Don Colburn
John Dulis
Chad Egger
Michael Evans
Aaron Furman
Pavel Gorbnov
Josh Harding

Will Harmon
Jeremy Harris-
Smith
Russell Herculson
T.J. Hodges
Debra Jarvis
Casey Jensen
Chris Jensen
Josh King
Bryan Klebon
Blair Knouse
Tereza Krejci
Adrian Kuder
Kyle Lankford
Nancy Lord
Bill Malchow
Micah Melton
Charlie Mitchell
Greg Morris
G. Lee Murdoch
Cliff Nichols
Tom Parent

Radek Pavlicek
Michal Pohl
Cory Polidore
Jon Reeves
Logan Rosenberg
Howard Rumbley
Rob Sample
Frankie Sears
Emerson Sklar
Peter Slachta
Josh Smith
John Speake
Bryan Stafford
Travis Sterling
Tom Sturtevant
Dana Teague
Ray Teat
Ryan Teat
Peter Telepovsky
Calvin Yelverton

2005

Adam Abruzzo
Dee Appler
Ray Appler
Wadde Barnes
John Bigony
Francis Boecker
Josh Boecker
Josh Bounds
Jim Brady
Paul Brady
Bob Bramble
David Bramble
Scott Cheesman
Taras Chorni
James Cook
John Dulis
Nikolay Erzhakov
Mike Evans
Anna Filippova

Matt Gonce
Pavel Gorbunov
Tom Hagin
Will Harmon
Jeremy Harris-Smith
Russell Herculson
Chris Jensen
Blair Knouse
Kyle Lankford
Nancy Lord
Jake Martin
Patrick McNamara
Kenny McVey
Micah Melton
Mitchell Melton
Ben Millman
Charlie Mitchell
Greg Morris

Lidia Okliyevch
Tom Parent
Aleksey Petrov
Logan Rosenberg
Morgan Rosenberg
Wayne Schmidt
Craig Scott
Emerson Sklar
Josh Smith
John Speake
Bryan Stafford
Travis Sterling
Dana Teague
Ray Teat
Ryan Teat
Maria Teshechko
Mike Thompson
Luke Twilley
Kenny Williams

2006

Nikolay Antonov
Dee Appler
Ray Appler
Ryan Batchelder
Francis Boecker
Josh Boecker
Chris Bounds
Jim Brady
Paul Brady
Bob Bramble
David Bramble
Matt Cathell
Scott Cheesman
Matt Ciriacy
James Cook
Ian Cotter
Paul Curtis
Mike Deal
Mikhail Desyatov
John Dulis
Bailey Elmore
Mike Evans

Tatiana Gluntsova
Aleksander Gorbulin
Dane Hartman
Brian Hayden
Russell Herculson
Chris Jensen
Tim Kemp
Blair Knouse
Cody McClellan
Kenny McVey
Micah Melton
Stacey Mertsalova
Ben Millman
Andrewy Milyutin
Charlie Mitchell
Greg Morris
Danny Neighoff
Tom Parent
Roger Peek
Mark Porches
Jill Price

Will Rooney
Logan Rosenberg
Morgan Rosenberg
Sergey Samarskiy
Frankie Sears
Dustin Shahan
Emerson Sklar
Josh Smith
Travis Sterling
Tom Sturtevant
Ken Swearingen
Dana Teague
Ray Teat
Ryan Teat
Shane Temple
David Theiss
Kyle Vestal
Brandon Wilkins
Kenny Williams
Matt Winebrenner

2007

Adam Abruzzo	Dane Hartman	Alex Sarahan
Dee Appler	Chris Jensen	Rob Scott
Ray Appler	John Kemp	Frankie Sears
Irina Batashova	Tim Kemp	Chris Seiss
Robert Batta	Blair Knouse	Bandon Sells
John Bigony	Travis Larmore	Colton Shaheen
Chris Bounds	Aaron Lehman	Alex Sharkey
Jim Brady	Zach Lehman	Josh Smith
Paul Brady	Jack McCann	Sergiy Smuchock
Bob Bramble	Brandon Mears	Andrew Solomon
David Bramble	Mark Mears	Kevin Sterling
Kevin Chalfont	Micah Melton	Travis Sterling
Scott Cheesman	Michell Melton	Tom Sturtevant
Victoria Chubuk	Matt Miriacy	Kara Teat
Don Colburn	Charlie Mitchell	Ryan Teat
James Cook	Todd Morgan	Paul Thornton
Ian Cotter	Greg Morris	Kyle Walker
Rob Dechene	G. Lee Murdoch	Sean Wenstrup
Tara DiGiovanni	Dan Neighoff	Brandon Wilkins
Jerold Dulis	Matt O'Sullivan	Ken Williams
John Dulis	Tom Parent	Matt Winebrenner
Mike Evans	Iroslav Roienko	
Nathan Evans	Morgan Rosenberg	

2008

Adam Abruzzo
Dee Appler
Ray Appler
Bobby Batta
J.R. Bigony
John Bigony
Chris Bounds
Paul Brady
Bob Bramble
David Bramble
Ethan Breslin
Kevin Chalfont
Scott Cheesman
Victoria Chubuk
Matt Ciriacy
Ian Cotter

Bob Dechene
Billy Draper
Greg Emerson
Sean Farrell
Chris Jensen
John Kemp
Tim Kemp
Blair Knouse
Adrianne Lego
Micah Melton
Mitchell Melton
Crystal Meredith
Greg Morris
G. Lee Murdoch
Danny Neighoff
Tom Parent

Bobby Richardson
Alex Sarhan
Jess Schimming
Rob Scott
Frankie Sears
Josh Smith
Alex Stinson
Tom Sturtevant
Ryan Teat
David Theiss
Kyle Walker
Sean Wensrup
Brandon Wilkins
Matt Winebrenner

2009

Zarina Battalova
Jon Bigony
Chris Bounds
Jim Brady
Paul Brady
Sam Brennan
Ethan Breslin
Andrew Carlson
Phillip Caruthers
Scott Cheesman
Don Colburn
Edie Crank
Hector Delgado
Will Detterline
Lisa Dianderth
Christian
DiBenedetto
Greg Emerson
Jonathon Evans
Nathan Evans
Sean Farell
John Gray
Jesse Greene
Michael Griffith

Russell Herculson
Sean Hidinger
John Howe
Chris Jensen
Emmanuel Johnson
John Kemp
Timur Khakimov
Michael Kibler
Jean-Paul Koushel
Taylor Larmore
Brandon Lawson
Mark Mears
Crystal Meredith
Brent Michell
Charlie Mitchell
Re'nato Moore
Todd Morgan
Millie Morris
G. Lee Murdoch
Brian Neighoff
Danny Neighoff
Kristina Nosova
Sean O'Connor
Matt O'Sullivan

Bobby Richardson
Jessica Rossi
Alden Ruben
Frankie Sears
Brandon Sells
Colton Shaheen
Emerson Sklar
Harry Smith
Andrew Solomon
Aristotle Stamat
Ryan Teat
Dave Theiss
Paul Thornton
Katelin Tull
Nate Valenti
Kyle Walker
Sean Wenstrup
Brandon Wilkins
Matt Winebrenner
Rafel Ziyatdinov
Alina
Angeliya
Natalya

2010

Michal Bachora
Russel Bailey
Alex Batta
Drew Batta
Chris Bounds
Paul Brady
Bob Bramble
Dan Breeding
Sam Brennan
Ethan Breslin
Scott Cheesman
Don Colburn
Edie Crank
Aleksander Czyz
Jordan Dennison
Will Detterline
Zach Ellis
Linda Engelhard
Michael Enis
Jonathon Evans
Mike Evans
Nate Evans
Sean Focht
Askhat
Galyautdinov

John Gray
Jesse Greene
Patrick Hamann
Karen Hardy
Matt Heitman
Jared Higgins
John Howe
Chris Jensen
Ethan Johnson
Tracie Johnson
Sean Jordan
Vasilisa Karpova
Blair Knouse
Krista Kolb
Jean-Paul Koushel
Taylor Larmore
Travis Larmore
Ginny Mattes
Crystal Meredith
Todd Morgan
Millie Morris
G. Lee Murdoch
Matt O'Sullivan
Jonathan Reel
Bobby Richardson

Thomas Richardson
Matt Ritter
Logan Rosenberg
Alden Rubin
Jess Schimming
Frankie Sears
Andrew Solomon
Aristotle Stamat
Kevin Sterling
Travis Sterling
John Stichberry
Hunter Tatum
Ryan Teat
Ben Tibbetts
Kyle Walker
Robert Wertz
Brooke Wheatley
Brandon Wilkins
Matt Winebrenner
Greg
Krystyna
Tom

2011

Steven Accocella
Kevin Bailey
Jesse Bartrum
Ora Bartrum
Mariola Bartczak
Alex Batta
Drew Batta
Tre Berry
Chris Bounds
Paul Brady
Matt Brault
Dan Breeding
Ethan Breslin
Caitlin Burroughs
Andrew Carlson
Don Colburn
Edie Crank
Brad Cullen
Aga Czarnocka
Marcus Davis
Jordan Dennison
Zach Ellis
Greg Emerson
Jon Evans
Nate Evans
Wojtec Glowacki
Jesse Greene

Karen Hardy
Jared Higgins
Shawn Horrocks
Jon Howe
Tommy Hudson
Chris Jensen
Carrie Johnston
Joe Jones
Sean Jordan
Nick Kelly
John Kemp
Cole Koester
Jean-Paul Koushel
Maura Kovalchik
Taylor Larmore
Travis Larmore
Tyler Littleton
Doug Martin
Micah Melton
Chrystal Meredith
Thomas Molter
Todd Morgan
Dan Morton
Sean O'Connor
Matt O'Sullivan
Marta Panska
Shawn Pierce

Anna Pogonowska
Mary Powers
Chanel Preston
Alex Ranken
John Reel
Bobby Richardson
Dan Sauers
Pete Schmaus
Andrew Solomon
Harry Stephens
Hunter Tatum
Josh Taylor
Ryan Teat
Bart Trebacz
Nathan Valenti
Spencer Valenti
Zach Wagamon
Kyle Walker
Rob Wertz
Matt Winebrenner
Kelson Wong
Scott Worsham
Nick Wright
Aleksander
Wybierala

2012

Andrew Albanese
Ed Anderson
Ora Bartrum
Jesse Batrum
Paul Brady
Matt Brault
Andrew Carlson
Don Colburn
Dave Collier
Edie Crank
Brad Cullen
Marcus Davis
Eric Decker
Brandon Dykes
Zach Ellis
Wojceich Glowacki
Tomasz Gniadek
Andrew Hidinger
Jared Higgins
Shawn Horrocks
Chris Jensen
Buck Jones
Joe Jones

John Jones
Nick Kelly
A.J. Kindschy
Jean-Paul Koushel
Maura Kovalcik
Joanna Kula
Taylor Larmore
Travis Larmore
Luke Leblanc
Jake Leonard
Doug Martin
Ginny Mattes
Matt McQueeney
Crystal Meredith
Mike Metcalf III
Angelika Milli
Thomas Molter
Todd Morgan
Sean O'Connor
Matt O'Sullivan
Vincent Peters
Anna Pogonowska
Mary Powers

Bob Richardson
Eric Salser
Dan Sauers
Pete Schmaus
Rebecca Schmaus
Urszula Skawska
Michal Sliwinski
Andrew Solomon
Harry Stephens
John Stichberry
Garrett Stokes
Tom Sturtevant
Hunter Tatum
Ryan Teat
Chris Valenti
Nate Valenti
Spencer Valenti
Matt Winebrenner
Kellson Wong-Williams
Scott Worsham

2013

Andrew Albanese
Alex Bates
Trevor Beachboard
Matthew Brault
Cameron Carpenter
Jimmy Chaparro
Don Colburn
Edie Crank
Eric Daniel
Darius Dashiell
Michael Deal
Michael Evans
Nathan Evans
Gabe Fauser
Erik Fehrenbacher
Jared Feldman
Cyndie Flowers
Michal Gnutek
Andrew Hidinger
Chris Jensen
Alex Jones
Buck Jones
Joe Jones
John Jones
Sean Jordan

Matthew Kasa
Matther Kinneer
Jean-Paul Koushel
Justin Lawson
John Libby
Dave Machinski
Jared Maule
Matthew McQueeney
Crystal Meredith
Michael Metcalf
Krzysztof Mezyk
Thomas Molter
Todd Morgan
Steven Morton
Billy Murdoch IV
Sean O'Conner
Patty O'Neil
Lukasz Pasternak
Maria Podlasinka
Mary Powers
Patty Powers
Josh Rawlings
Alex Ray
Eric Salser

Dan Sauers
Ceaser Skiis
Nick Smith
Andrew Solomon
Jason Staley
Harry Stephens
Garrett Stokes
Joanna Swida
Avery Tarrant
Jack Tawes
Ryan Teat
William Theis
Harry Tralongo
Daniel Twilley
Kinga Tworzydlo
Christopher Valenti
Brandon Veasey
Lauren Wertz
Scott Worsham
Nick Wright
Bernie Yanos
Mary Yanos
Michael Young
Darren Youse

2014

Adam Abruzzo
Kevin Bailey
Chris Barth
Kenny Baxter
Paul Behe
Alec Bowers
Mark Browne
Cameron Carpenter
Jimmy Chaparro
Edie Crank
Eric Daniel
Darius Dashiell
Sandy Davis
Paul Derepentigny
Joe Elarde
Justin Elarde
Mike Evans
Erik Fehrenbacher
Will Fehrenbacher
Jim Ford
Johnny Garcia
Kurt Godfrey
Eric Goins
Alex Gray
Ilonka Grzesiak

Robert Hoopes
Chris Jensen
A.J. Jones
Buck Jones
Dylan Jones
John Jones
Jan Kubczak
Taylor Larmore
Justin Lawson
John Libby
David Machinski
Nicholas Machinski
Cameron Maule
Jared Maule
Andrew May
Crystal Meredith
Kaitlin
Middlebrooks
Monica Mohr
Aiden O'Connor
David Olmstead
Mary Powers
A.J. Ravert
Bob Reese
Craig Richards

Edward Rowe
Kuba Sakowski
Eric Salser
Dan Sauers
Taylor Saunders
Valarie Shorter
Ryan Siverson
Eric Siverson Jr.
Nick Smith
Steve Smith
Andrew Solomon
Garrett Stokes
Jared Sullivan
Mycah Sykes
Jack Tawes
Ryan Teat
Harry Tralongo
Daniel Twilley
M.J. Vaughn
Brandon Veasey
Zach Wagamon
Lauren Wertz
Scott Worsham
Nick Wright
Kuaudia Zalega

2015

Russell Bailey
Kenny Baxter
Alec Bowers
Christina Bowie
Eric Bowmaster
Justin Breidenbach
Cameron Carpenter
James Chaparro
Grzesiu Ciuba
Jake Condron
Edie Crank
Eric Daniel
Paul Derepentigny
Jacqueline Dockins
Erik Fehrenbacher
Will Fehrenbacher
Seth Feldman
Trever Fisher
Joshua Graham
Ilonka Grzesiak
Vincent Hammerer
Nathan Hoffman

Miguel Iglesias
Vincente Iglesias
Chris Jensen
Alexander Jones
John Jones
Tomek Karst
Jake Lahoff
Justin Lawson
Tom Leitz
David Machinski
Nick Machinski
Matthew Malone
Andrew May
Crystal Meredith
Thomas Molter
Greg Morris
Grayson Murray
Patrycja Naklicka
Aiden O'Connor
Hayden Olmstead
Gavin Petersen
Craig Richards

Ania Rudolf
Dan Sauers
Taylor Saunders
Frankie Sears
Virginia Sears
Ryan Siverson
Nick Smith
Andrew Solomon
Jared Sullivan
Avery Tarrant
John Tawes
Ryan Teat
Harry Tralongo
Spencer Valenti
M.J. Vaughn
Richard Webster
Lauren Wertz
Liam Williams
Nicholas Wirth
Scott Worsham
Scout, camp dog

2016

Jarad Alpert
Noah Andres
Kyle Benbrook
Bartek Blazkow
Alec Bowers
Christina Bowie
Eric Bowmaster
Cameron Carpenter
Jimmy Chaparro
Joseph Chojnacki
Edie Crank
Eric Daniel
Paul Derepentigny
Darrell Dill
Marcellus Dockins
Brandon Donovan
Rebekah Donovan
Erik Fehrenbacher
Seth Feldman
Aga Giermasz
Sam Hokins
Phil Hudson

Miguel Iglesias
Vincente Iglesias
Chris Jensen
John Jones
Aaron Koenig
Asia Kozlowska
Jake Lahoff
Justin Lawson
Przemek Lubecki
David Machinski
Nick Machinski
Matt Malone
James May
Andrew McKee
Mitch Miller
Cierra Mohr
Ted Mullin
Brauch Murray
Aiden O'Conner
Jeanine Ordoyne
Devon Raickle
Craig Richards

Kindall Ridgely
Dan Sauers
John Schermerhorn
Emerson Sklar
Nick Smith
Andrew Solomon
Jared Sullivan
Magda Szulc
Avery Tarrant
John Tawes
Ilonka Teat
Ryan Teat
Clifford Terell
Harry Tralongo
Spencer Valenti
Richard Webster
Kyle Wells
Harley Werner
Scott Worsham
Beatrix, camp dog
Budd, camp dog
Scout, camp dog

2017

Jarad Alpert
Shannon Anderson
Noah Andres
Kyle Benbrook
Christina Bowie
David Bramble
James Chaparro
Regina Cheesman
Scott Cheesman
Joseph Chojnacki
Zachary Clendenin
Jacob Collins
Aldon Conley
Edie Crank
Cole Cropper
Luke Crowhurst
Eric Daniel
Erik Deckert
Paul Derepentigny
Darrell Dill
Marcellus Dockins

John Dulis
Beata Gadowska
Aga Giermasz
Kayla Gore
Aaron Gray
Jonathan Harris
Sam Hopkins
Phil Hudson
Miguel Iglesias
Chris Jensen
Jake Lahoff
Przemek Lubecki
Nicholas Machinski
Andrew Martin
Andrew May
James May
Andrew McKee
Kaitlyn Mills
Alex Mohr
Gavin Petersen
Charles Pollard

Paden Radunske
Devon Raickle
Craig Richards
Dan Sauers
John Schermerhorn
Alex Simonetti
Ryan Siverson
Emerson Sklar
Andrew Solomon
Steve Stokes
Jared Sullivan
Alicja Sztubecka
Ryan Teat
Will Theis
Tom Vebeliunas
Kyle Wells
Evan Williams
Liam Williams
Scott Worsham

2018

Jacob Adkins
Jarad Alpert
Jordan Ball
Ian Berry
Christina Bowie
David Bramble
Isaiah Brinsfield
Jimmy Chaparro
Antnie Chojnacki
Joseph Chojnacki
Christy Clendenin
Matthew Coleman
Nicholas Coleman
Jacob Collins
Aidon Conley
Paul Derepentigny
Darrell Dill
Marcellus Dockins
John Dulis

Dalton Facer
William Fachet
Aaron Gray
Sylwia Hachula
Phil Hudson
Miguel Iglesias
Chris Jensen
Maria Kolodziejczyk
Przemek Lubecki
James May
Andrew McKee
Kaitlyn Mills
Alex Mohr
Dawid Olender
John Phillips
Charles Pollard
Devon Raickle
Sean Raickle

Craig Richards
Dan Sauers
Wesley Schaire
Alexander Simonetti
Emerson Sklar
Andrew Solomon
Randall Stafford
Keegan Stever
Jared Sullivan
Ryan Teat
Kevin Teter
Tomas Vebeliunas
Kyle Wells
Evan Williams
Liam Williams
Suzi Williams
Scott Worsham

2019

Jacob Adkins
Ale Alarcon
Perry Beachum
Kyle Benbrook
Christina Bowie
David Bramble
Isaiah Brinsfield
Carla Carrizales
Jimmy Chaparro
Antnie Chojnacki
Joe Chojnacki
Christy Clendenin
Nicholas Coleman
Matthew Coleman
William Cotton
Paul Derepentigny
James Derepentigny
Darrell Dill
Marcellus Dockins
Kate Fachet

Will Fachet
Robby Fetterman
Matthew Gilmour
Aaron Gray
Jacen Horne
Phil Hudson
Chris Jensen
Brendan Kelly
Kamil Kotlik
Jennifer Larsen
Nick Machinski
Justin Marx
Jim May
Jonathan Ornelas
Stephen Payne
John Phillips
Virginia Phuong
Sean Raickle
Devon Raickle
Craig Richards

Dan Sauers
Edward Schaefer
Wesley Schaire
Alex Simonetti
Emerson Sklar
Randall Stafford
Keegan Stever
Steve Stokes
Jared Sullivan
Bartlomiej Taska
Ryan Teat
Kevin Teter
Suri Valencia
Dalton Wayne
Isiq Williams
Liam Williams
Suzi Williams
Gerry Wood
Scott Worsham

Part Six:
References

Acknowledgements

This book would not be possible without the support of the Del-Mar-Va Council, Boy Scouts of America, and its staff and volunteers.

Special thanks are owed to all of the Scouts, Scouters, volunteers, summer camp staff members, and supporters who generously contributed their time sharing stories, memories, photographs, and records. Their recollections and reminiscences were vital in piecing together five decades of camp history.

A significant part of this book is drawn from the original research and writings of the late Dr. Ken Gerlach, who penned the original 1996 manuscript outlining the history of the early camp and the names of the campsites, trails and outposts. I have edited and condensed some of his work for simplicity's sake, but left the majority intact. To Dr. Gerlach, whose love of Nanticoke spanned the decades, we owe a debt that can never be repaid.

I am thankful for the love and support of my wife, Rachel Kipp, for putting up with my drives to Sharptown and puttering around on this project. Our children – Dassi, Mateo, and Liam – also exhibited great patience with their dad's strange obsessions.

Memory can be a tricky thing, fading in some parts and bright and vibrant in others. This book relies in large part on memories of decades ago, and represents their recollections as faithfully as it can.

Dan Shortridge

Sources Consulted

Interviews

I am incredibly grateful to the following campers, Scouters, and staff members who shared their time, memories, photographs, and stories for this book:

Clifford Alpert, Ray Appler, Chris Arbeene, Jim Barber, Ray Bertrand Jr., Francis Boecker, Seth Braunstein, Adam Brooks, Scott Cheesman, Henry Clifford, Don Colburn, Zadock Cropper, Christopher Cullen, Rob Dechene, Paul DeRepentigny, John Dulis, Buck Duncan, Mark Dyer Sr., Jeff Faust, George Fleckenstein, Aaron Furman, Michael Gallagher, Chris Gonzalez, Alexander Hawthorne, Greg Hill, Chris Jensen, Rob Kuklewicz, Patrick Lenz, David Machinski, Roger Maki, Rob Malone, Rick Meinersmann, Micah Melton, Lee Murdoch, Keith Olds, Jill Price, Eric Salser, Charlie Shaeff, Chandler Sickmund, Seiji Sugiura, Wayne Stacey, Bill Sterling, Gene Sterling, Kevin Sterling, Ray Teat, Ryan Teat, David Thiess, and Scott Worsham.

Articles

The following newspaper and publication articles, listed in chronological order, helped reconstruct the history of much of the early years of camp.

"Rhoads retires as Scout head." The Morning News (Wilmington, Del.), April 3, 1957.

"Record Attendance Looms For Rodney Scout Camps." The Morning News (Wilmington, Del.), June 3, 1958.

"Camp Sought Down State." The News Journal (Wilmington, Del.), June 24, 1959.

"Del-Mar-Va Scout Executive Named." The Delmarva News (Selbyville, Del.), August 27, 1959.

"29 Scout Troops to Open Rodney Camping Season." The Journal-Every Evening (Wilmington, Del.), June 24, 1960.

"Boy Scout Camp Attendance Hits New High." The Daily Times (Salisbury, Md.), July 21, 1961.

"Boy Scout Camp Site Optioned." The News Journal (Wilmington, Del.), November 20, 1961.

"Boy Scouts Get Options On Land For Shore Camp." The Daily Times (Salisbury, Md.), November 20, 1961.

"New Camping Facilities Needed by 17,000 Scouts." The Daily Times (Salisbury, Md.), November 28, 1961.

"Scout Council Seeks $1,500,000 For New Expansion of Facilities." The Daily Times (Salisbury, Md.), December 8, 1961.

"Wayne Pump Makes First Gift To Scout Fund." The Daily Times (Salisbury, Md.), March 2, 1962.

"Central Shore Scout Camping Site Purchased." The Daily Times (Salisbury, Md.), March 18, 1963.

"Del-Mar-Va Scout unit sets 3 goals." The Morning News (Wilmington, Del.), March 16, 1964.

"Nanticoke Scout Reservation to be ready by July 11." The Morning News (Wilmington, Del.), November 26, 1964.

"Scout Reservation To Open July 11." The Evening Journal (Wilmington, Del.), November 27, 1964.

"New Nanticoke Scout Reservation To Open." The Daily Times (Salisbury, Md.), June 16, 1965.

"New Nanticoke Scout Reservation Is Dedicated." The Daily Times (Salisbury, Md.), July 19, 1965.

"Millsboro Scouts Weekend At Camp." The Delmarva News (Selbyville, Del.), July 29, 1965.

"Nanticoke Scout Camp Is Given Recognition." The Daily Times (Salisbury, Md.), August 16, 1965.

"Scouting Builds Leaders Through United Fund Aid." The Daily Times (Salisbury, Md.), October 15, 1965.

"Area Scout membership up 4.4 pct." The Morning News (Wilmington, Del.), February 11, 1966.

"Scout Camping Starts Sunday." The Evening Journal (Wilmington, Del.), June 22, 1966.

"Scouts Set For Camping Season." The Daily Times (Salisbury, Md.), June 22, 1966.

"Lost Scout Is Found Safe On Nanticoke Reservation." The Daily Times, Salisbury, Md., July 26, 1966.

Associated Press. "400 Search For Boy Scout Who Wasn't Lost At All." The Daily Mail (Hagerstown, Md.), January 26, 1966.

"Danish Teacher Working At Wicomico Scout Camp." The Daily Times (Salisbury, Md.), July 25, 1971.

"Youth Found Dead at Scout Camp." The News Journal (Wilmington, Del.), July 11, 1972.

"Airmen Help To Spruce Up Scout Camp." The Daily Times (Salisbury, Md.), October 27, 1974.

Cunningham, Paul. "Japanese Scout Counselor Helps Out At Shore Camp." The Daily Times (Salisbury, Md.), August 10, 1975.

"Eagle scout." The Morning News (Wilmington, Del.), June 25, 1976.

"Canadian Scouts Camp At Nanticoke." The Daily Times (Salisbury, Md.), July 18, 1976.

"Scout Executive Is Leaving Post." The Daily Times (Salisbury, Md.), November 29, 1976.

"Scout Honored." The Daily Times (Salisbury, Md.), April 2, 1979.

Robinson, Bill. "Boy Scouts Gather At Camp Nanticoke." The Daily Times (Salisbury, Md.), May 5, 1982.

"Obituary: William H. Cantara." The News Journal (Wilmington, Del.), February 6, 1984.

"Campmasters meet." The Star-Democrat (Easton, Md.), August 22, 1984.

"Scouts Present Silver Beaver Awards." The Daily Times (Salisbury, Md.), November 14, 1984.

Stegman, Carolyn. "COPE course challenges students." The Daily Times (Salisbury, Md.), April 7, 1966.

Gerstel, Susan. "Henson Receives Citizen's Award." The Daily Times (Salisbury, Md.), May 11, 1986.

"Sussex District Names Top Scouting Family." The Daily Times (Salisbury, Md.), April 10, 1987.

Dean, Gail. "Building character: Camp Nanticoke gives Scouts a taste of outdoor life." The Star-Democrat (Easton, Md.), July 17, 1986.

"Gift Is Presented." The Daily Times (Salisbury, Md.), January 18, 1988.

"Teat Is Reservation's Resident Director." The Daily Times (Salisbury, Md.), July 11, 1988.

"New Building." The Daily Times, August 10, 1989.

"Training Is Held." The Daily Times (Salisbury, Md.), February 12, 1990.

"Boy Scouts go to camp." The Star-Democrat (Easton, Md.), July 18, 1990.

Duck, Bill. "Nature is his office: Ray Teat is resident director at Henson Scout Reservation Camp Nanticoke." The Daily Times (Salisbury, Md)., August 4, 1991.

DeCourcey, Jim. "Scouts aid in tree-saving efforts." The Daily Times (Salisbury, Md.), December 31, 1992.

"Death Notices: J. Shepherd 'Shep' Henry, 78." The Daily Times (Salisbury, Md.), February 24, 1993.

Fooksman, Leon. "Ray Teat appointed to school board." The Daily Times (Salisbury, Md.), August 4, 1994.

Dean, Gail. "Commitment to education leads Teat to spot on Dorchester board." The Star-Democrat, August 26, 1994.

Teat, Ray. "Core knowledge lays learning foundation." The Daily Times (Salisbury, Md.), February 16, 1996.

Kraemer, Nicole, and Jon Bentz. "Police find lost Scout." The Daily Times (Salisbury, Md.), July 4, 1997.

Morse, Dan. "Boy Scout, 13, survives 32 hours mired in swamp." The Baltimore Sun (Baltimore, Md.), July 5, 1997.

Shortridge, Dan. "Camp Nanticoke expansion complete." The Daily Times (Salisbury, Md.), July 2, 2000.

Lavender, Chris. "Scouts preserve Henson Scout Reservation from development." The Star-Democrat (Easton, Md.), January 27, 2005.

"Ehrlich announces purchase of conservation easement." The Kent Island Bay Times (Chester, Md.), March 2, 2005.

"Murdoch is new director at camp." The Star-Democrat (Easton, Md.), November 19, 2006.

"Walam Olum Hokum," Archaeology magazine, 2009. Accessed https://archive.archaeology.org/online/features/hoaxes/walam_olum.html.

"Boy Scouts break ground on camp." The News Journal (Wilmington, Del.), September 18, 2011.

Historical Resources

The following articles, books and manuscripts were cited in Ken Gerlach's original 1996 history of the early years of camp. In some cases, the citations are incomplete and precise details have been unable to be determined. Records of correspondence and telephone interviews cited are similarly unavailable.

Austin, Frank. "A Tentative Report on the Willin Site (18-DOR-1)." The Archaeolog 19, no. 2 (Oct 1967): 1-32.

Coursey, Cecile A. Private communication to C.W. Dayton Jr. 9/12/79.

Coursey, Cecile A. Telephone interview. 14/29/96.

Davidson, Thomas E. "Historically Attested Indian Villages of the Lower Delmarva." Maryland Archaeology 18, no. 1 (Mar 1982): 1-8.

Davidson, Thomas E. "Where are the Indian Towns?" Journal of Middle Atlantic Archaeology 1 (1985): 43-50.

Dayton, C. W. Jr. The Higgins-Menke Site, Goose Point, Chancellor Point Road, Talbot Co. Md. Unpublished report to the Maryland Archaeological Society, Mar 1986.

Dean, Gail. "Sandy Hill: The Dig of 1927" (interview with Judge Wm. B Yates II). Banner: Leisure Section. 17 Feb 1984: 2-5.

Dragoo, Don W. "Adena and the Eastern Burial Cult." Archaeology of Eastern North America. Ann Arbor: Braum-Brumfield. Vol. 4 (winter 1976): 1-9.

Ehrlich, Arlene. "The Right to Rest in Peace." Baltimore Sun Magazine. 22 Oct 1989: 8-13. (Includes interview with Nause- Waiwash Chief Sewell Fitzhugh.)

Fausz, J. Frederick. "Present at the Creation: The Chesapeake World That Greeted the Maryland Colonists." Maryland Historical Magazine 79, No. 1 (spring 19814): 7-20.

Fitzhugh, Sewell. Four-part series on the Indians of the Eastern Shore. Banner. Oct 1991: "The Nause and the Chicone and those that came before us." / "Meeting of two worlds: the English colonists and the natives." / "Blending of two communities: the Indian culture in Dorchester County." / "The re-emergence of Indian pride in Dorchester County."

Fitzhugh, Sewell. Telephone interview. 14/30/96.

Flegel, Perry S. "Choptank and Nanticoke Pottery Differences." The Archaeolog 31, no. 1 (summer 1979): 14-8.

Flegel, Perry S. "The Marshyhope Creek, Its Indian Places, Pottery, Points, and Pipes." The Archaeolog 30, no. 1 (summer 1978): 13-59.

Flegel, Perry S. "Who Were the Choptank Indians?" The Archaeolog 31, No.1 (summer 1979): 1-3.

Flowers, Thomas A. Dorchester County, Maryland, A History for Young People. Cambridge, Md.: Flowers, 1982.

Ford, T. Latimer Jr. "Adena Sites on Chesapeake Bay: Sandy Hill Site (18D030) Dorchester County Maryland." Archaeology of Eastern North America 4, winter 1976: 76-89.

Gerlach, George K. The Marshyhope Legends. 1964-1965. Unpublished manuscript.

Huelle, Walter E. Footnotes to Dorchester County History. Cambridge, MD: Tidewater.

Jones, Elias. New Revised History of Dorchester County Maryland. Cambridge, MD, 1966: 181-188.

Marye, William B. "Indian Paths of the Delmarva Peninsula; Part 2: The Choptank Indians." Bulletin of the Archaeological Society of Delaware, October 1937.

McCallister, James A. Jr. (compiler). Indian Lands in Dorchester County: Selected Sources 1669 to 1870. Unpublished, 1962.

McCutchen, David (translator and annotator). The Red Record: The Wallam Olum. New York: Avery, 1989.

McNamara, Joseph M. "Excavations on Locust Neck: the Search for the Historic Indian Settlement in the Choptank Indian Reservation." Journal of Middle Atlantic Archaeology. Vol 1 (1985), 87-95.

Mowbray, Calvin W. "Mystery Surrounds the First City Survey." Banner, 1993, 2.

Mowbray, Calvin W. "Two Surveys Were Made of Choptank Indian Reservation." Banner, October 23, 1993: 14.

Porter, Frank W. III. "Behind the Frontier: Indian Survivals in Maryland." Maryland Historical Magazine 75, no. 1 (March 1980): 42-54.

Porter, Frank W. III. Indians in Maryland and Delaware. Bloomington: Indiana University Press, 1979: 20-26. Seabrease, Wilsie G. The Nanticokes and Other Indians of Delmarva. Easton: Seabrease, 1969.

Speck, F. G. Indians of the Eastern Shore of Maryland. University of Pennsylvania Press, 1922.

Weslager, C. A. The Nanticoke Indians - Past and Present. Newark: University of Delaware Press, 1983.

Wissler, Clark. Indians of the United States. New York: Doubleday, 1940, 1966. Yates, William B. II. Telephone interview, April 1996.

--------. Proceedings of the American Philosophical Society 87 (1944): 398-402.

--------. Handbook for Boys. New York: Boy Scouts of America: 1911 (32nd printing, 1940).

--------. Webster's Biographical Dictionary. Springfield: Merriam, 1943.

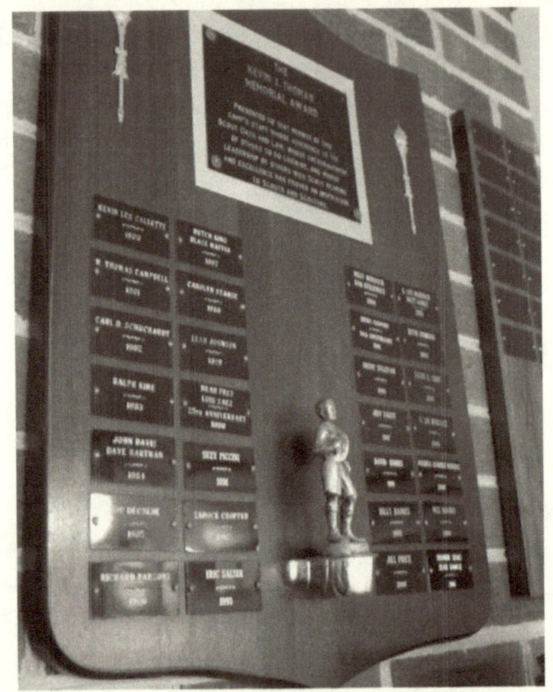

The Kevin J. Thomas Award

The Kevin J. Thomas Memorial Award, given since 1980, is presented to that member of the camp's staff whose adherence to the Scout Oath and Law, whose encouragement of others to do likewise, and whose leadership of others with Scout bearing and excellence has proved an inspiration to Scouts and Scouters.

A staff member in 1977 and 1978, Thomas was the son of Council Camping Director Max C. Thomas and his wife, Dorothy Thomas. He passed away of cancer at age 22 in 1979. His father was a district executive in Del-Mar-Va Council, scout executive at the Anthracite Council, and U.S. Air Force retiree. He also served as camp director at Rodney Scout Reservation.

Two staff members have received the award twice: Lee Murdoch in 2001 and 2004 and Matthew O'Sullivan in 2010 and 2012.

1980 **Kevin Les Callette**

1981 **W. Thomas Campbell**

1982 **Carl D. Schuchardt**

1983 **Ralph Kime**

1984 **John Davis,**
     Dave Hartman

1985 **Bob Dechene**

1986 **Richard Parsons**

1987 **Butch King, Blase Maffia**

1988 **Carolyn Stange**

1989 **Leah Johnson**

1990 **Brad Frey, Luis Saez**

1991 **Suzy Piccini**

1992 **Zadock Cropper**

1993 **Eric Salser**

1994 **Billy Murdoch,**
Rob Kuklewicz

1995 **Henry Clifford**

1996 **Brent Sullivan**

1997 **Jeff Faust**

1998 **David Harris**

1999 **Billy Haines**

2000 **Jill Price**

2001 **Lee Murdoch, Matt Gonce**

2002 **Kevin Sterling**

2003 **David R. Chew**

2004 **Lee Murdoch**

2005 **Josh Bounds**

2006 **Will Rooney**

2007 **Frankie Sears,**
     Blair Knouse

2008 **Ray Appler**

2009 **Paul Brady**

2010 **Matthew O'Sullivan**

2011 **Micah Melton**

2012 **Matthew O'Sullivan**

2013 **Andrew Solomon**

2014 **Mike Evans**

2015 **Alex Jones**

2016 **Aaron Koenig**

2017 **Scott Cheesman**

2018 **Paul DeRepentigny**

2019 **Isaiah Brinsfield**

The Deed

The original deed for the camp was recorded on May 9, 1963, between Francis and Bessie Holloway of Salisbury and the Del-Mar-Va Council.

BOOK 132   476

THIS DEED, made this -9th- day of May, in the year nineteen hundred and sixty-three, by Francis L. Holloway and Bessie C. Holloway, his wife, of Wicomico County, and State of Maryland, witnesseth:

THAT in consideration of the sum of Five Dollars ($5.00), and other good and valuable considerations, the receipt of which is hereby acknowledged, the said Francis L. Holloway and Bessie C. Holloway, his wife, do hereby grant and convey unto The Del-Mar-Va Council, Inc., (Boy Scouts of America), a body corporate of the State of Delaware, all of those tracts, pieces or parcels of land situate, lying and being between the Nanticoke River and Red Bank Road, or the road which leads through the property owned by Elmer Rathel from the Sharptown-Eldorado State Road, in the First or Fork Election District of Dorchester County, Maryland, and described as follows, that is to say:

FIRST

ALL that tract or parcel of land which was conveyed as Tract or Parcel No. 1 in a deed unto the said Francis L. Holloway and Bessie C. Holloway, his wife, by William P. Coopersmith, widower, by deed dated the 15th day of September, 1959, and recorded among the Land Records of Dorchester County, Maryland, in Liber P. L. C. No. 116, Folio 213, in which said deed the said tract of land is therein and herein described as follows: " 'Tract or parcel No. 1: All those parts or tracts of land called 'Buck Hill' and 'Phillips Regulation' Beginning for the outlines of the same at a stone and post set up at the south end of the division line between the land hereby conveyed and the Benjamin McWilliams land, thence North 65½ degrees East, 14.61 perches; North 71½ degrees East, 139 perches or until it comes opposite a division fence between the land hereby conveyed and William M. Wheatley's Land; thence with the same, North 23 degrees West, 137 perches, to a post or corner of the said Benjamin McWilliams land; thence with the same South 58-3/4 degrees West, 5 perches to the beginning of the above referred to division line; thence with the same South 18½ degrees East, 61-3/10 perches to the place of beginning, containing 47 acres of land, more or less' ", Saving and Excepting, all that lot or parcel of land which was conveyed therefrom by the said William P. Coppersmith, and Emma H. Coppersmith, his wife, unto Russell E. Coppersmith and Francis I. Coppersmith, his wife, by deed dated February 16, 1948, and recorded among the aforesaid Land Records of Dorchester County, Maryland, in Liber R. S. M. No. 65, Folio 392, which said lot fronts 200 feet on the southerly side of the public road leading to Red Bank, together with the buildings and improvements thereon.

For further title of the herein named grantors in and to said land and property, see deed unto them from Jonathan E. Wheatley and wife, dated the 15th day of January, 1960, and recorded among the aforesaid Land Records of Dorchester County, Maryland, in Liber P. L. C. No. 117, Folio 576.

SECOND

ALL those tracts or parcels of land which were conveyed unto the said Francis L. Holloway and Bessie C. Holloway, his wife, as tenants by the entireties, by Elmer Allen Cox and Edith C. Cox, his wife et al., in a deed dated the 23rd day of November, 1959, and recorded among the aforesaid Land Records of Dorchester County, Maryland, in Liber P. L. C. No. 117, Folio 121, in which

HARRINGTON & THOMPSON
ATTORNEYS AT LAW
CAMBRIDGE, MARYLAND

BCOK 132 477

said deed said lands conveyed therein are herein also likewise described as follows:

"No. 1: All that tract or part of tract or parcel of land, Beginning for the same at the southeast corner of land now owned by the grantees but formerly belonging to William P. Coppersmith and hereinafter referred to as the Coppersmith land, (being the tract of land herein conveyed as First), it being the northeast corner of the land hereby conveyed, and running thence (1) by and with the said Coppersmith land, South 78 degrees and 30 minutes West, a distance of 2145 feet; thence (2) South 34 degrees and 30 minutes West, a distance of 600 feet; thence (3) South 20 degrees 00 minutes East, to the Nanticoke River; thence, (4) beginning for the fourth course at the point of beginning of this description and running thence South 20 degrees 00 minutes East, by and with the property of Elmer Rathel, a distance of 2400 feet, more or less, to the Nanticoke River, with a frontage on said Nanticoke River of approximately 2750 feet, containing 140 acres of land, more or less."

"No. 2: All the lots or parcel of land designated as Lot No. 1 and Lot No. 2, in deed dated April 4, 1938, by J. Gorman Hill, Trustee, in No. 5893 Chancery, to Jonathan Wheatley of Dorchester County, who is one of the grantors herein, which deed is now of record among the said Land Records of Dorchester County in Liber J. F. D. No. 37, Folio 522; and

"No. 3: All other cripple lands heretofore owned by the grantors herein lying to the westward of the said State Road leading from Sharptown to Eldorado and between the said Red Bank Road and the said Nanticoke River, it being the purpose and intention of the grantors to convey to the grantees all cripple lands owned by the grantors, located as aforesaid, although they may not be specifically described herein; and there is included and intended to be conveyed herein without exception or reservations, all that piece or parcel of land patented to Arthur Hill by the Province of Maryland on the 20th day of September, 1741, as 'Neighborly Kindness' now of record in Liber E. I. No. 6, Folio 407, in the Office of the Land Commissioner of Maryland, Annapolis, Maryland, and laid down therein as containing 110 acres of land, more or less, and is the piece or parcel of land patented as 'Neighborly Kindness' and described in deed to G. E. H. Wheatley, father of Jonathan E. Wheatley, one of the grantors herein, from Patience Walker, et al., dated January 13, 1935, and now of record in Liber R. S. M. No. 105, Folio 348, one of the Land Record Books of Dorchester County, Maryland."

TOGETHER with the buildings and improvements thereupon erected, made or being; and all and every, the rights, alleys, ways, waters, privileges, appurtenances and advantages to the same belonging or in anywise appertaining.

TO HAVE AND TO HOLD the land and premises above described and mentioned, and hereby intended to be conveyed; together with the rights, privileges, appurtenances and advantages thereto belonging or appertaining unto and to the proper use and benefit of The Del-Mar-Va Council, Inc., (Boy Scouts of America), a body corporate of the State of Delaware, as aforesaid, its successors and assigns, in fee simple.

AND the said Francis L. Holloway and Bessie C. Holloway, his wife, hereby covenant that they will warrant specially the property hereby granted and conveyed; and that they will execute

BOOK 132   478

such other and further assurances of said land as may be requisite.

WITNESS the hands and seals of said grantors.

TEST:

Elnora McCafferty
Elnora McCafferty
As to both

Francis L. Holloway   (SEAL)
Francis L. Holloway

Bessie C. Holloway   (SEAL)
Bessie C. Holloway

STATE OF MARYLAND, Wicomico County, to wit:

I Hereby Certify, that on this -9th- day of May, in the year nineteen hundred and sixty-three, before me, the subscriber, a Notary Public of the State of Maryland, in and for the County aforesaid, personally appeared Francis L. Holloway and Bessie C. Holloway, his wife, the within named grantors, known to me, to be the persons whose names are subscribed to the within and foregoing deed, and acknowledged that they executed the same for the purposes therein contained.

Witness my hand and Notarial Seal:

Elnora M
Elnora McCafferty,
Notary Public

Received for Record: MAY 10 1963 Rec. No. 20299
Dorchester Co. - Clerk *Philip L. Cannon*

The Maps

The camp trail map dates back to the 1960s, with the original map drawn up by Ken Gerlach and his team of volunteers. The campsite map was developed to provide a more detailed view of the central camp area and help direct Scouts and leaders to their sites.

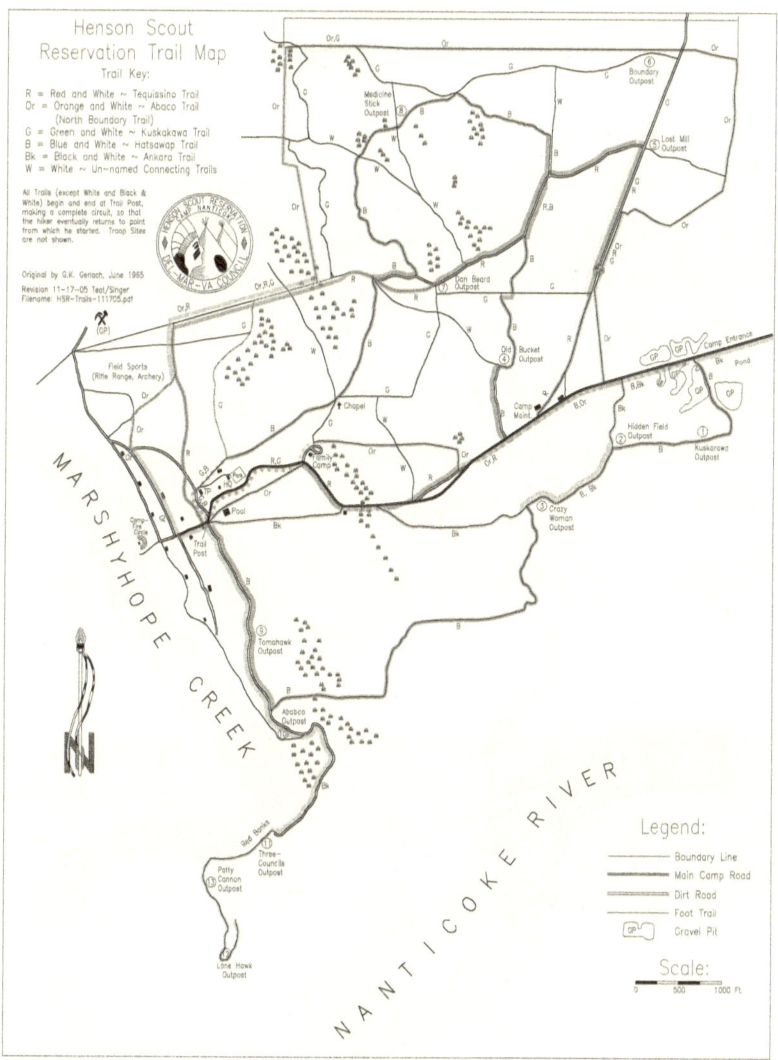

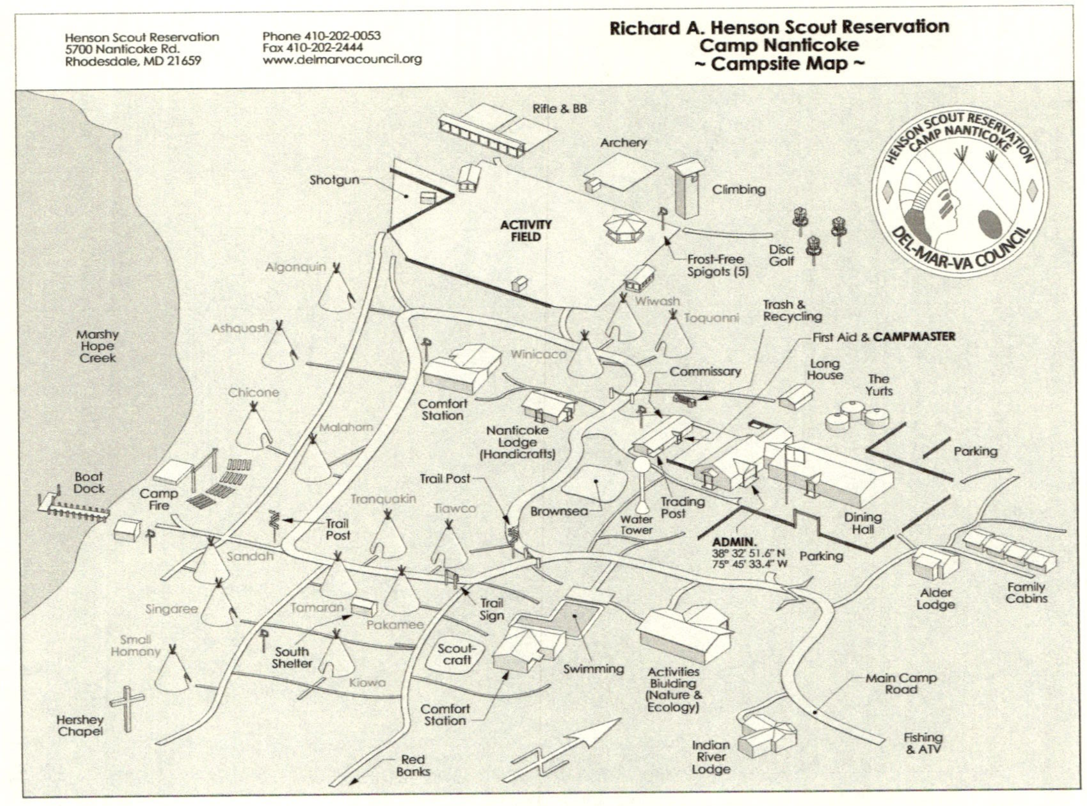

Henson Scout Reservation
5700 Nanticoke Rd.
Rhodesdale, MD 21659
Phone 410-202-0053
Fax 410-202-2444
www.delmarvacouncil.org
Richard A. Henson Scout Reservation
Camp Nanticoke
~ Campsite Map ~
HENSON SCOUT RESERVATION
CAMP NANTICOKE
DEL-MAR-VA COUNCIL
Rifle & BB
Archery
Shotgun
Climbing
ACTIVITY FIELD
Frost-Free Spigots (5)
Disc Golf
Algonquin
Wiwash
Toquanni
Trash & Recycling
First Aid & CAMPMASTER
Marshy Hope Creek
Ashquash
Winicaco
Commissary
Long House
The Yurts
Chicone
Comfort Station
Nanticoke Lodge (Handicrafts)
Parking
Boat Dock
Malaham
Trail Post
Brownsea
Water Tower
Trading Post
Dining Hall
Camp Fire
Tranquakin
Tiawco
ADMIN.
38° 32' 51.6" N
75° 45' 33.4" W
Parking
Trail Post
Sandah
Alder Lodge
Family Cabins
Singaree
Tamaran
Pakamee
Trail Sign
Small Homony
South Shelter
Scout-craft
Kiowa
Swimming
Activities Biulding (Nature & Ecology)
Main Camp Road
Comfort Station
Hershey Chapel
Red Banks
Indian River Lodge
Fishing & ATV

About the Authors

Dr. G. Kenneth Gerlach (1931-2008) was Scoutmaster of Troop 188 in Cambridge, Md., from 1958 to 1972, and a driving force behind the creation of the Nanticoke Scout Reservation. He laid out and cut trails and developed the official map during 1964 and 1965. He served as camp program director at in 1965 and 1966, and as camp commissioner in 1972 and 1975. He also served as a district commissioner, was a recipient of the Silver Beaver, and was a member of the Order of the Arrow.

Outside of Scouting, Dr. Gerlach served as principal of several schools in Dorchester County, Md., retiring in 1989. In 1996, he published "On the Naming of the Campsites, Trails and Outposts, Richard A. Henson Scout Reservation, 1964-1996," the seminal history of the early camp years, which part of this book draws upon. He passed away on June 23, 2008.

Dan Shortridge fell in love with Camp Nanticoke in the mid-1980s, when he first visited as a Cub Scout running in Sussex District's chariot races. As a Boy Scout, he camped here for four summers and worked on staff for five, serving as a CIT, assistant commissioner and Scoutcraft director. A Vigil Honor member of the Order of the Arrow, he has been a district volunteer and troop committee chair. He has worked in public relations and marketing and is a former newspaper editor and reporter. His writing has been published or will appear in Camping, CampBusiness, and Parks and Recreation Business magazines. He lives in Camden, Del., with his wife and three children.

For this book, he revised Dr. Gerlach's original manuscript, researched the history of the camp and local Scouting, gathered stories and memories from more than 50 people, and wrote new material to continue the Nanticoke story.

Friends of Scouting

Each week, more than 12,000 Scouts across the Delmarva Peninsula raise their hands and make a promise. It's more than just a pledge to an organization. It represents a lifelong commitment to them and to the community they share.

It takes another kind of promise – the one inside themselves – to help them grow into productive adults. That is what Scouting on Delmarva is all about. Help us fulfill that promise by becoming a Friend of Scouting.

Friends of Scouting (FOS) is the Del-Mar-Va Council's annual giving campaign encouraging businesses, community leaders and corporations to make a monetary investment in Scouting.

You can make your donation at www.delmarvacouncil.org or by calling 302-622-3000.

Thank you for your consideration and support of Scouting's ability to change lives.

Henson Staff Alumni Association

The Henson Staff Alumni Association (HSAA) was formed in 2020 to support Henson Scout Reservation through the cultivation and preservation of the culture of and relationships amongst staff alumni. The goal of HSAA will be to collaborate for the betterment of the reservation through staff development, programmatic support, and financial support.

Your membership and support will help that cause. Annual memberships are $50, which will include quarterly newsletters, invitations to HSAA events, and opportunities to give back to Henson in ways other than financially. Additional membership levels come with benefits including patches and special recognition in camp.

Register as a member by visiting the HSAA's donation page at https://donations.scouting.org/#/council/081/appeal/3081.